Czech Political Prisoners

Czech Political Prisoners

Recovering Face

Jana Kopelentova Rehak

LEXINGTON BOOKS
Lanham • Boulder • New York • Toronto • Plymouth, UK

All photographs © Jana Kopelentova Rehak.

Published by Lexington Books
A wholly owned subsidiary of The Rowman & Littlefield Publishing Group, Inc.
4501 Forbes Boulevard, Suite 200, Lanham, Maryland 20706
www.rowman.com

10 Thornbury Road, Plymouth PL6 7PP, United Kingdom

British Library Cataloguing in Publication Information Available

Library of Congress Cataloging-in-Publication Data

Rehak, Jana Kopelentova, 1968-
  Czech political prisoners : recovering face / Jana Kopelentova Rehak.
    pages cm
  Includes bibliographical references.
  ISBN 978-0-7391-7634-4 (cloth : alk. paper) — ISBN 978-0-7391-7635-1 (ebook)
  1. Political prisoners—Czechoslovakia—Case studies. 2. Political persecution—Czechoslovakia—History—20th century. 3. Victims of state-sponsored terrorism—Czechoslovakia—Case studies. 4. Czechoslovakia—Politics and government—1945-1992. I. Title.
  HV9660.3.R44 2013
  365'.4509437090345—dc23
                                                                      2012039066

∞™ The paper used in this publication meets the minimum requirements of American National Standard for Information Sciences—Permanence of Paper for Printed Library Materials, ANSI/NISO Z39.48-1992.

Printed in the United States of America

Contents

Preface

This book is the story of men and women who survived Czechoslovak Communist concentration camps. Men and women disappeared, were arrested, imprisoned, interrogated, tortured, put on trial, convicted, and sentenced to forced labor camps. In Czechoslovakia between 1948 and 1989, *political others* became political prisoners.

New forms of political practices developed under the institution of the totalitarian Czechoslovak Communist state. This new regime of totalitarian political power produced culturally specific forms of organized political violence, and the political power of the state was constituted in ritualized forms of violence. Between 1948 and 1989 some citizens recognized by the state as political others were subjected to ritualized political violence. The link between ritualized violence and state subjects' political passage laid the groundwork for the formation of new social identities.

In the post-totalitarian state, political others from the socialist era remain others through their distinct desires and acts of coming to terms with the experience of organized violence. Like other members of the Czech and Slovak states, former prisoners are now facing the post-totalitarian remaking of their lives. In contrast to society at large, the political prisoners' recovery from the totalitarian past has proved that the ethics of political life, individual and communal coming to terms with the past, is closely related and crucial to their efforts towards reconciliation.

Today, in the Czech Republic, as well as in other post-socialist countries, the desire to reconcile is not limited to survivors of camps, prisoners and dissidents. People from the younger generations are asking questions about crimes, punishment and forgiveness related to the Communist regime in Central and Eastern Europe.

The purpose of this book is to expose individual and communal experiences, subjectivity and consciousness hidden in the ruins of memories of socialism in Czechoslovakia.

Acknowledgments

This book is based on the support, advice, friendship, and hospitality of many people in the Czech Republic and the United States. Thank you to Lexington Books for their interest and their efforts in publishing this book. Especially, thank you to Amy King and the staff of Lexington Books for their work.

This book was supported by several organizations. American University in Washington, D.C., provided me with a Vollmer Foundation Scholarship in 2005. The American Fund for Czech and Slovak Relief in New York City provided me with an important fieldwork grant in 2003. The Dusti Bonge Foundation supported the photographic work, which accompanies this publication. The Czech and Slovak Heritage Association of Maryland, with great generosity, supported me in the final stages of this book and funded the publishing costs. Thank you to all these organizations for their kind support. I especially thank Margaret Supik, president, and the board members of the Czech and Slovak Heritage Association for all you have done. Without your support I would not have been able to finalize the publication of *Czech Political Prisoners: Recovering Face*.

In the United States a number of people helped me with their tremendous generosity and their belief in my continuing my work. Special thanks go to Ken Ackerman and Geoffrey Burkhart for their endless labor of reading my manuscript and for providing me with intellectual inspiration and support for this book. I want to thank Veena Das and Gyanendra Pandey for their intellectual generosity and the Anthropology Department of Johns Hopkins University for providing me with an invitation to an intellectually inspiring environment. Thanks go to Gretchen Schafft for reading my first drafts and all her support in the early stages of this book. Thank you to all my friends who helped me in the process. Thanks go to Linda Vlasak, Martin Holub, Chris Ruff, and Amanda Konradi.

In the Czech Republic my fieldwork would have not been possible without the generosity of my informants who shared their life stories with me and allowed me to use them for my research. I would have remained an outsider to the prisoners' community if it were not for a number of individual prisoners, with whom I developed friendships. I thank them. Thanks go to all the spouses and children of prisoners for all their contributions.

I am grateful to many friends and to my parents for helping me to continue my fieldwork. In the process I benefited greatly from conversations about this research with Czech scholars, intellectuals and social-life analysts, especially Jiří Pehe, Jacques Rupnik, and Marie Ruth Križková.

I could never have written it without the tremendous help, encouragement and many sacrifices from my husband, Frank Rehak, and my daughters, Frances and Ester Rehak. Thank you, Frank, Frances, and Ester.

Part I

LOSING FACE

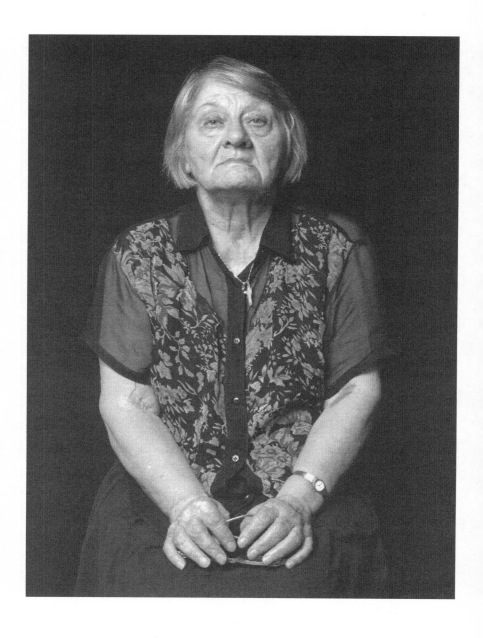

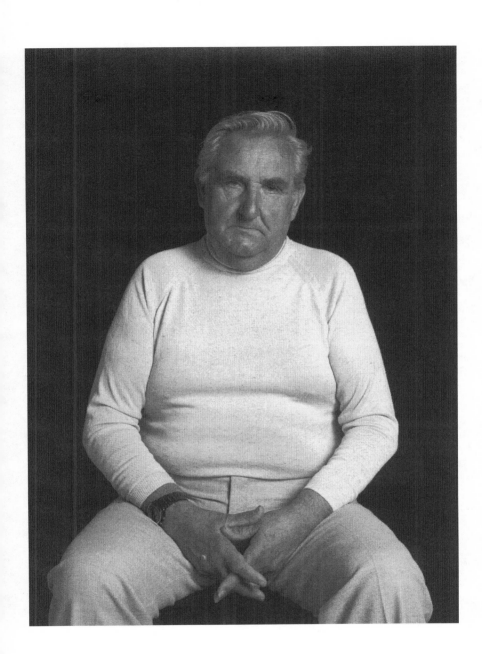

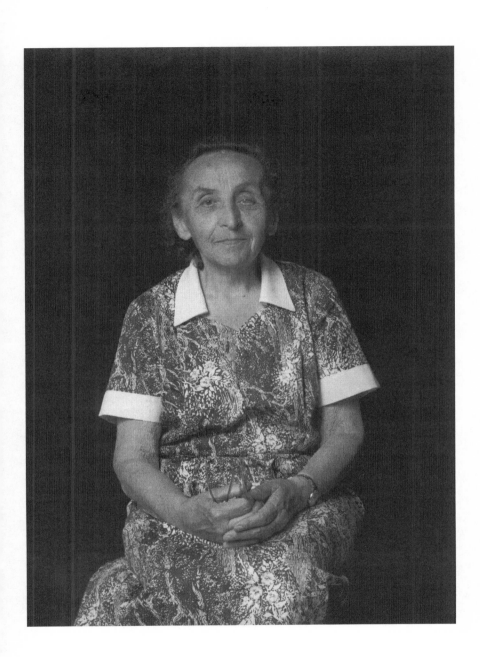

Chapter One

Owners of Pain

All living beings are in the open: they manifest themselves and shine in their appearance. But only human beings want to take possession of this opening, to seize hold of their own appearance and of their own being manifest. Language is this appropriation, which transforms nature into face. This is why appearance becomes a problem for human beings: it becomes the location of a struggle for truth.

—Agamben (2000:90)

SUNDAY RITUAL

In the summer of 1995 I found myself in Prague looking closely at the faces of people on the streets. I asked myself questions about their, our, memories of the oppression under socialism. I lived in the Czech Republic until 1994, when I left for the United States. During my first return, in the summer of 1995, while sitting one Sunday morning in Café Ganys, I noticed a small group of older men who were sitting around one table drinking coffee or wine. The questions I had been asking myself about faces in the streets and my memories came to rest on them; I wanted to find out who they were. At first they reminded me of my grandfather, who, as I remember from my childhood, used to come every Sunday to our town, Sušice, to the town square. From midmorning until noon, he and the other elders would talk as they moved back and forth between the square and the pub. It was their Sunday ritual. While some wives and children went to church or were cooking Sunday lunch, the men carried out their ritual. In the Czech family, Sunday lunch is a big, warm meal, and compared to other days of the week, not an ordinary lunch. Sunday lunch is traditionally the only time when the family will share a meal with outsiders. This recollection of Sunday morning rituals in a small town in Southwest Bohemia piqued my curiosity about those men I saw in Prague. I wondered, who are they? Why are they sitting here? What is their connection to one another?

As my curiosity grew, I went over to their table, introduced myself and asked about the reason for their gathering. I asked them who they were and what brought them together. They first looked at each other with uncertain expressions on their faces. Then one of them said: "We worked together, a long time ago." After that a second man said: "We worked together in uranium mines, in the fifties." I was interested to know more about them. They invited me to join them and began to tell me how they met in the work camps during the 1950s. I was told they were Mukls or Muklyněs—men or women selected for liquidation (in the Czech language, *Muž určený k likvidaci*). In 1948 the StB (State Secret Police) had arrested them and sentenced them to prisons and labor camps. After World War II they, like many Czechoslovak citizens, were not ready to passively accept the Soviet model of political power and were actively involved in anti-Communist and Soviet resistance.

That Sunday morning I learned from their brief stories that their lives had been controlled by the state until 1989. Between 1948 and 1989 some citizens designated by the state as political others were subjected to ritualized political violence. The survivors call themselves Mukl(s), and I learned that they met in this café every Sunday morning between 9 a.m. and noon. I was informed that the number of participants changed based on the seasons, but on any given Sunday around ten men attended.

I returned the following Sunday, and our conversation about their experiences continued. I learned further that many among the Mukls were partisans, soldiers who fought against the Nazi army or survivors of Nazi prisons. The soldiers fighting during the Second World War on the western front were among the most organized, radical anti-Communist political others. Mukls in their narratives indicated that the protective tendencies found among many Czechoslovak citizens after the war were not the products of nationalistic tendencies but rather of political feelings, of fears influenced by their experiences with the Nazi occupation of Czechoslovakia.

My Sunday conversations with Mukls led me to read related historical accounts, novels and memoirs. I became familiar with the historical context of their arrests and the years that followed. I learned further that after the defeat of Nazism in Europe the boundaries of states were reestablished and new forms of political power over Central Eastern Europe were formed. Soviet control of political and economic life eventually included the control of many aspects of Czech and Slovak lives (Hejl and Kaplan 1986). Many Czechoslovaks silently conformed to new political power structures, and some resisted.[1]

The group of older men I met at Ganys belong to part of a population who had been resistant to the new politics of the state. As a photographer and ethnographer meeting Mukls, I was struck by not just the legacy of the violence they had faced, but also how it marked their faces and became their voice. Face, as I see it, is a powerful means of communication which possesses the potential to restore social visibility. In this context, Mukls' lost face, made invisible by the regime, always held the possibility for recovery. I became interested in learning their individual stories and asked if I could photograph them. They agreed, and so on the third Sunday, I found an unused separate room in the café and asked the manager if I could use this place as a photographic studio. He agreed and I set up my camera, tripod, black background, and two lights.

I realized much later that the making of their portraits was the best and easiest way for me to connect with the Mukls on a deeper level. Not only was I trained as a photographer, but also I am a third-generation photographer. My grandfather had a photographic studio in my hometown, and my father continued the tradition. My family lost their business to the Communist regime in 1948 and was forced to work for a collective, which was directed by their former competitor. In the late 1960s, when the political atmosphere relaxed, my father was offered work with the city cooperative in a newly built studio. He hired my grandparents in addition to other people and, ironically, the cameras and equipment they worked with were mostly ours, confiscated after 1948. It was a significant part of my childhood to watch my grandfather and father photographing people from the town and surrounding villages. This was the era of black-and-white photography when photographic technology was not widely available to ordinary people. My grandfather and my father knew about lighting and about face. They always found the words to engage their subjects, strangers and people they knew. For me their studio was a space where I learned to relate to strangers while photographing them. Knowledge of the craft of photography was important as was experience dealing with people. This personal exposure was formative for my professional identity and the work strategies I adopted later. That is why I find photographing strangers natural even at the first contact, and why I asked the men in the group to come individually into this improvised studio to be photographed.

They came, and I made over a dozen portraits of each person. When photographing, I asked them to sit on the chair and face the camera directly. I made portraits of five or six men, all of who agreed to meet for individual interviews. My apartment was located in the center of Prague, in the same neighborhood as Café Ganys, and they were comfortable meeting me there.[2] I never interviewed individual Mukls at Ganys, but I often made notes during group meetings there. During that summer I recorded twelve individual narratives, and I photographed the narrators.

I knew at this point, in 1995, that this was a story, visual and written, that I wanted, even needed to tell. While I still could not see the shape it would take, I continued to collect data with an increasingly focused sense of the story I wanted to tell, the record I wanted to present, and the form that the data I had collected would allow me to construct. I realized then that though their narratives were about the past, their memories were constituted in the present, and these were memories of pain that I needed to communicate.

I listened and interjected comments only when my informants became silent. My verbal commentary during the narratives tended to encourage and advance the telling. Over time, as I began to notice recurrent perceptions, I became more systematic in note taking. These notes became useful during my later work when developing the outline for this book. I also received several handwritten or typed narratives from Mukls who could not meet with me for various reasons or had heard about my interests and my project from friends and chose to participate indirectly. In 1996 I recorded more interviews, now with both men and women former political prisoners, to learn how women prisoners' experiences differed from those of men prisoners. Women prisoners responded differently. Many refused to talk or did not want to be recorded; several agreed to meet only in groups. My first interview with women prisoners was a group of six that I met at their monthly meeting held in the small salon of a Prague restaurant.[3] They came to my apartment[4] and shared their stories in community with other women prisoners. Following this group interview I met with other women prisoners during my fieldwork. While the women were, in general, more reticent at first than the men, when they did engage in narratives, they were more specific than the men about some subjects. For example, in their torture and pain narratives, they spoke more openly about intimate aspects of their experiences, especially concerning their solidarity in prison. They articulated their pain and togetherness in different ways than the men.

In addition to meeting with Muklyněs, I continued conducting individual interviews with Mukls, not in my apartment, but now in the central office of the Confederation of Political Prisoners.[5] Mukls I knew from Ganys introduced me to others who did not participate in the Sunday Ganys meetings. I spent two months visiting the central office of Confederation of Political Prisoners conducting over thirty interviews and photographic sessions with individual Mukls. Only a few Mukls I met through the Confederation refused to participate. Most Mukls wanted to tell their story.

I was also invited to Mukls' homes to record their narratives. Home interviews were usually more fragmented, reflective and longer than interviews conducted in my apartment or those done at the Confederation office. These longer and less structured interviews proved helpful in my efforts to understand the context of the Mukls' recent lives. Home interviews also became the foundation for enduring relationships with particular Mukls, friendships through which I could reconnect with Mukls when I returned to Prague.

Between 1995 and 2004, I conducted individual interviews, which I recorded and later transcribed. These interviews range in length between one and two hours. I recorded or wrote up these sessions as notes, depending on the circumstances of the interview. I translated a number of them into English, but later worked with transcriptions in Czech. After I recorded some of the narratives, I followed up with informal conversations. On these occasions I tended to ask open-ended questions based on the Mukls' earlier narratives, though focused on several general themes: the process from arrest through release, experiences in the camps, relationships to family, and eventually reconciliation. I treat reconciliation as a dialogic process of multiple forms of recovery from the violent past, but also acknowledgment of a subject's pain. Such acknowledgment of pain is not limited to individual injury, it also legitimizes the collective quest for repair, revitalization, and healing. What is meant by repair is not just healing, but transformation to a different moral state. In my reconciliation narratives, I emphasize the problematic notions of truth. I have used the term *fictive* to refer, as some others have (Arendt 1966, Feldman 2001, Taussig 1999, Ross 2001), to complexities and multiple levels of the impact of violence on specific social groups such as Czech political prisoners.

Eventually, after I had been wrestling with the flow of Mukls' narratives for three or four years and searching for a coherent construction of their experience, I realized the importance of the succession of events, first arrest, then interrogation, and finally trial. From 1995 to 2006, in Prague, I collected ethnographic data on the Mukl experience. I recorded Mukls' stories as they remembered them and made individual photographic portraits of them. Overall, I am connecting a variety of data—life history narratives, observations of social gatherings and participant observations of the Mukls' everydayness. Life histories and informal talks with individual Mukls were recorded, while data from participation in social events and small informal gatherings are based on my note taking during or after the events. I also kept a journal while in the field which became an additional source.

The way Mukls began their narratives varied. Some talked immediately about their resistance to the Communist government in 1948. Others asked me specifically what I wanted to know about. In the latter case I would ask, "What effect did the events of 1948 have on the life you were leading at that time?" The narratives took different directions. The cohesion and fluency of

Mukls' narratives varied from person to person. Some spoke about life in the work camps and others spoke about the fate of different family members. Some told their story in a calm voice. Other narratives were fragmented by emotional distress evoked by memories of difficult moments in the camps or the process of separation from country and family. This often occurred when Mukls spoke about harassment of their children or parents by the regime or when they spoke of torture.

Mukls often spoke about their families in multiple terms: loss and fragmentation, a vehicle for punishment and pain, but also a source of emotional empowerment. Their voices reveal a dramatic change in family life in Czechoslovakia. The nuclear family, highly significant in the Czechoslovak context, was reconstituted under the influence of the political events of the 1950s. In a climate poisoned by distrust and fear, sharp divisions between public and private space, and shifts in the configuration of kinship relations began to appear.

Between 1997 and 2004, I returned to the Czech Republic for several months each year to collect more ethnographic data, as well as archival data such as legal documents, photographs, prisoners' journals, music, poetry, and novels. The project currently encompasses sixty-seven recorded interviews with single informants,[6] thirty-five portraits of members of the prisoner community, and documentary photographs of official prisoner meetings, memorial rituals and informal gatherings. In addition, I have interviewed prisoners' relatives, specifically seven children and ten spouses. Above all, I paid extra attention to the Mukls' family. I was anxious to know more about their social interactions in the present. I asked, "What does it mean to belong to a Mukls' family now, in the post-socialist period?"

In the early stage, when I focused almost exclusively on individual Mukls' narratives, I asked questions directed by my interest in the formation of Mukls' subjectivity. Each narrative followed a similar time line: pre-arrest, arrest, interrogation, trial, imprisonment, return, but each differed in how much was said about these shared topics.

Fieldwork done in 2003 focused mainly on Mukls' social interactions which led to more interviews with Mukls' spouses and children. The 2003 fieldwork was significant for this project in that I had become a participant. I noticed that Mukls take me for an insider within the Mukl community. I tried to increase the number of Muklyně informants, but, as was the case almost from the beginning of my research, I found them more resistant to interviewing, although more expansive when they did provide information about their experiences. With the exception of Milu, whom I knew before I began this work, it was much more difficult for me to make contacts with former women prisoners. Even after participating in a number of the women's monthly meetings in Prague, I was more successful in becoming part of the Mukls' community than in becoming part of the Muklyněs' community.

I focused on Muklhood as lived today, Mukls' communal life, and on the experiences of Mukls' spouses and children. After the intentional separation resulting from arrest followed by imprisonment of different members of a family, Mukls established different ways of belonging to a new family—the Mukl family. Such a family not only provided a new and alternative location for belonging, but also became a new, redefined relatedness supplanting what was lost to the violence. The social dynamic of this newly established union included a strong sense of connectedness, care, and solidarity among prisoners. Life in the camps was harsh and dehumanizing, and yet the darkness, as they recall it in the communal setting, was full of surprising humor. I was moved by this interesting shift in prisoners' relatedness indicating an expansion of notions of family.

In 2003 I also met a number of new informants in two locations: at Jáchymov (a small town and labor camps location) and at the Milada Horáková Club[7] in Prague. At Jáchymov I reconnected with Mukls from Prague, and I was introduced to Mukls I had not yet met. During one weekend I recorded the recollections of members of this group of Mukls as they walked through the campgrounds. They were younger than the Mukls I knew from Prague. This new contact led to an invitation to the next Mukls' annual gathering at Šternberk castle in the town of Český Šternberk. Mukl Zdeněk Šternberk has organized annual celebrations for a small group of Mukls in his restituted castle. I participated in this weekend gathering. The event was important in increasing my understanding of Mukls' social life today and for meeting more members from the Mukls' community outside the Prague circle.

I also researched new memorial and archival sites, newly published literature, and recent media presentations of political prisoner discourse. I studied documents and visual materials archived in the Museum of *Třetího odboje* (The Third Resistance) in the city of Příbram. These include letters and diaries written by prisoners, photographs, objects made by prisoners while incarcerated and documentary films made after 1989. Also in this archive are documents from 1968 regarding the rehabilitation of the prisoners. They are from the Academy for the Investigation of Crimes of Communism, *Ústav pro vyšetřování zločinů komunismu.*

In comparison to other Czech citizens, Mukls are a more homogeneous group because of their shared experience of violence. But underneath that homogeneity, Mukls are individuals with varying degrees of identity. The process of recovery in post-socialism is closely tied to its historical context. The rituals of violence against those deemed to be political others led to the formation of a new Mukls' community. The unifying basis for Mukl identity includes opposing a totalitarian state and subsequently being punished formally by that state. The persons punished came to their opposition from different educational, political and religious backgrounds and social classes. For some, the experience of Muklhood became the defining experience of their lives. It is through this group that I have come to my understanding of the formation and consequences of the making of and becoming a Mukl. After hearing individual testimonies from Holocaust survivors, Langer (1991) realized that assumptions about shared memory and collective consciousness cannot be simply the domain of universalistic notions of suffering. My informants and I cannot claim to speak for all Mukls and Muklyněs. Yet, it is both the gross similarities in their experiences and in the life consequences of those experiences that allow me to use this means to tell their story.

This work is based on fieldwork among Mukls living in Prague.[8] The core of my male informants branched out from the small group of friends I met at Ganys. Through them, the group of my informants was enlarged by introductions to other Mukls. The latest fieldwork (2003–2005) focused on the expression of Mukls' social life. I observed their social events and their mutual relatedness in everyday situations. My investigations of Muklhood evolved from a focus on the formations of individual Mukls' subjectivity and moved towards the Mukls' communal language of reconciliation today. Coming to terms with the past while remaking their world after the experience of violence, and coping with the disruption caused by that violence, are both part of the process of reconciliation.

Many whom I interviewed stated that no one is interested in their story today, or that the evil they experienced remains unpunished. They often expressed deep disappointment in their failure to achieve justice after the fall of the Communist regime. The reconciliation process for Mukls has been closely tied to the judicial system, and, as a result, questions regarding the role of law in the context of a totalitarian state are important to consider.

ETHNOGRAPHIC REPRESENTATION

I write from the place where Mukls' and my politics overlap. I also share their desire to reconcile or come to terms with the past in totality. I was born in the spring of 1968, in Sušice, a small town in southwest Bohemia, shortly before the Soviet army invasion of Czechoslovakia.[9] Since my family was considered dangerous by the state and was always observed by state police, I was exposed to the duality of social life growing up as I did during *Normalizace*. The double character of social life during Normalization is a theme discussed by many Czech dissident writers, in particular Václav Havel. In the context of

Normalization, Havel often emphasized in his writing the tension between the Communist Party's political messages and the passive, conscious conformity of many citizens.

From the Mukls' point of view, their individual and social experiences of Czechoslovak political life during the 1950s is very different from their experiences after 1968. For many outsiders, political life under the Czechoslovakian Communist Party was translated by a generation of underground intellectuals from their post-1968 perspective. While I am not engaged in an analysis of the difference between Mukls and dissidents, it is important to understand that intellectual works produced by dissidents are not reflective of the Mukl experiences. Mukls do not identify with the experiences of political prisoners incarcerated during the period of Normalization between 1968 and 1989, nor is there a clear indication that the post-1968 dissidents identified with Mukls. In their narratives Mukls emphasized differences between conditions in Communist prisons during normalization and those they experienced in work camps and prisons of the Stalinist period. Generally Mukls see their experiences as political others as different from political others identified by the state after 1968.

In my life during Normalization, this duality was present in the gap between life within the family and life in public. For example, at home I was taught a different history and different values compared to those taught at school. My childhood was marked by an understanding that there are two variations of reality—private and public. Later, in my teenage years, I learned that anything I might say outside of my family home could be used against me or my family as justification for harassment. I was never interrogated, but my father was. On several occasions, as I recall, my father was also given the order from the police to stay home. This house arrest was related to political events. I also remember that in our town there was an undercover police agent in charge of my father; he was my father's personal *estébák* (StB agent).

The experiences of life under the political phase called Normalization, which I share with Mukls, influenced my methodology. As an insider I could ask research questions formed by my sympathy with the Mukls' struggle, by my care for Mukls' voices, and by my commitment to participate in their recovery from experienced violence. This position is methodologically challenging. I have had to be conscious of the tension between questions that are rooted in shared assumptions and questions that emerged from my analysis of Muklhood discourse. In retrospect, I realized that during the summer of 1995, I had begun doing what Joan Vincent has called politically engaged ethnography.

In the early stages of my research I focused on the Mukls' individual experiences. Later I began to recognize a shared identity which I will discuss as togetherness. In the final stages of my research, I realized that the Mukls' sense of community, alternative family, was fragmented by various forces. This led me to think about the relationship between the individual and his community in the context of ethnographic representation. Moving from individual life stories to the investigation of the Mukls' community allowed me to see their forms of relatedness, but also let me realize how, despite their own sense of belonging to the Mukl family, their individual experiences alienate them from everyone else.

My analysis of data has been strongly influenced by some of the ethnolinguistic methods of analysis of text. Based on focused coding I began to see patterns in the Mukls' speech. These patterns revealed more than just factual information; they contain multiple meanings or "intertextuality" (Bakhtin 1996) and an important domain of language, "double register" (Bakhtin 1996).

Analysis of the data is also tied to the development of my research questions which changed as this project evolved. I originally asked: What does political prisoners' remembering through their narratives reveal about the mechanisms of repression, punishment, alienation, and violence? Later in the process I asked: What are their new notions of relatedness? How do political prisoners relate to the outside world, family, friends, and society at large? How do they relate to each other? What is their relationship with the state in contrast to nation or motherland? What are their notions of social belonging? In the final stage of my fieldwork and in the period of writing up, I asked: What are the desired forms of reconciliation within the political prisoner community in the context of the post-Communist, contemporary Czech Republic's expressed national desire to belong to a modern Europe?

Anthropological writing, as I see it, can be creative and experimental; for example, ethnographic storytelling. Unlike "judicial models of witnessing" (Das and Kleinman 1997:26), storytelling is not directed toward problem solving. "Ethnographies can only take us to resting points that are not endings, but openings to new issues that require the continuous working through, so characteristic of everyday life" (Das and Kleinman 1997:26). I view the production of knowledge about violence by the mediators and translators of collective and individual violence in the mode of storytelling. My goal is to construct creative ethnographic narratives. I write based on my participant observation, formal and informal talks, and readings from Mukls' writings, but also from a politically engaged position.

The historical period of the 1950s in Czechoslovakia has been documented by a number of historians and commented on by political scientists. It has also inspired philosophers, playwrights, filmmakers and writers concerned with specific forms of Czechoslovak totalitarianism and the life of people under such political orders. In this context I ask: What does particular knowledge based on ethnographic data and an anthropological perspective, as informed by instances of violence, offer in a cross-cultural context? What then is the role of ethnography at the moment of transformation in studies of violence?

Mukls' faces, recorded by my camera, I hope will represent a form of reconciliation in which I can participate. Visual imagery is another way to tell a story, a different way from written narratives. The picture maker makes technical and methodological decisions that are different from those of the writer of a research text. Visual and written storytelling mutually reinforce the opportunity to communicate expressed pain and the strength of the voice desiring acknowledgment. As I see it, the connection between visual and written storytelling is in the restoration of denied agency.

When I returned from fieldwork and began to organize my data, new and old, it become clear to me that this project is not simply an archaeology of Mukl memory. When sorting through my fieldwork data, I asked many questions, but I kept coming back to the question of how to conceptualize related-ness under oppressive violence, how to show specific instances of the Mukls' constructions of subjectivities in the context of anthropological works which address the impact of violence elsewhere.

Memory, vision, language, time, and place are instrumental concepts for my interpretative analysis of temporality, fictive and secret political power embodied not only in Mukls' everyday experience, but also in particular events. Emerging from recent ethnographic works is a theoretical frame-work within which anthropologists examine political life in the context of the cultural production of violence. The ethnography of violence examines the collective experience of violence as well as individual negotiations with violent acts.[10] The works of scholars of the ethnography of violence share such themes as subjectivity formations, the fictive forces of political power, structural violence, the passage in space of death, transnational production of violence, violent events, ordinary instances of violence affecting social relatedness, and the process of recovery, re-claiming lost face or remaking the world after violent conflicts. These analytical concepts are developed with a diachronic dimension—concern with change. The notion of everydayness is understood as the site of the ordinary, and one of the central concerns is how people pursue their daily lives after life is transformed by the engagement with violence.

Drawing from my own ethnographic data, I have asked similar questions and employed similar analytical categories, concepts or themes developed within the new ethnography of violence. I see my work connected to these anthropological encounters with political life as part of a dialog about notions of subjectivity, time and place, language, memory, and pain in the context

of state terror. Such notions are embodied in the Czech Mukls' subjectivity formations and in their language of reconciliation. I want to add another
dimension to the anthropological discussion on subjectivity. In my project I
have sought to relate Czech Mukls' experiences of becoming Mukls and their
own sense of subjugation to political fiction. I included in my investigation
various modes of subject formations. I argue that the early formations of
Mukls' subjectivities and state violent practices developed symbiotically. The
political others, through political violent rituals, became political prisoners.

In examining the Mukls' narratives, I have drawn upon the Subaltern
Scholars' conceptualization of the subaltern's experience, and in particular
the "violations creating the structures of power" (Das 1997). Subaltern studies established the centrality of the historical moment of rebellion in understanding the subalterns, the inferiors, as the subjects of their own histories.
The Subaltern group treats specific historical events as texts in which can be
read the newly developing structures of power within the older power structures. Especially relevant to my work is how subaltern status is examined in
relation to the ruling elite (Guha 1999, Pandey 1991), how building a new
nation or state impacts on the category of family (Chatterjee 1993), and the
concept of recovering the subaltern voice and memory through the archive
(Guha 2000, Pandey 2001). Reading works of Shahid Amin, Ranajit Guha
and Gyanendra Pandey gave me insight into the potential of the archive,
memory, and figures of speech. The idea of memory as an alternative and
available archive, as discussed by Ranajit Guha, Gyanendra Pandey and other
members of the Subaltern School became critical for the formation of my understanding of figures of speech, consciousness and the formation of subject.

The patterns of violence in Mukls' narratives emerging from three distinct
events: arrest, interrogations and trial, led me to the concept of state violent
ritual. That led to the construction of what I came to understand as Mukls'
subjectivity, perhaps the essential element in the making of Muklhood. I refer
to subjectivity in the way Veena Das and Arthur Kleinman do in their writing
on the social suffering and production of local forms of violence. For them,
"subjectivity—the felt interior experience of the person that includes his or
her positions in a field of relational power—is produced through the experience of violence and the manner in which global flows involving images,
capital, and people become entangled with local logics in identity formation"
(Das and Kleinman 2000:1). In order for the political other to become a Mukl,
he or she had to undergo a passage through the state-directed violent rituals
of arrest, interrogation, and trial. Inspired by Veena Das's thoughts on pain
in the context of violent events (Das 2007), and also by Das and Kleinman
(2000), Desjarlais (1992) and Susanna Trnka (2008), I see pain, embodied
in prisoner's relatedness. I examine Mukls' pain in relation to their kin and

discuss how the pain of the others shaped newly developing cultural forms. Drawing from works on state violent rituals by Allen Feldman (2001), and on social defacement by Michael Taussig (1987), I conceptualize these Mukls' passage, critical for subjectivity formation, as an experience with the simulation of death, a passage through the "space of death" (Das 1997, Feldman 2001, Taussig 1987, 1999). Next to the older theoretical tradition of ritual of Leach (Leach 1964), Turner (Turner 1969), and Gluckman (Gluckman 1965), anthropologists concerned with ritual and political life, I held on their mutual ideas based on the assumption that we cannot separate the elements of ritual from the larger context.

One condition of these Mukls' rituals was the strategic isolation of the prisoner from society and family. I show how prisoners responded to such strategic isolation. The isolation produced the "social invisibility" (Poole 1997) of citizens who were considered enemies of the state. Such invisibility is felt by the prisoners as a "defacement" (Taussig 1999) or "loss of face" (Das 1995). Throughout their narratives and in different contexts Mukls spoke of instances of defacement. Those who were arrested immediately became invisible and remained so as long as they were being held, a form of defacement in both the public and private perception. In my analysis of Muklhood I use the term *ritual* to encompass state violent acts used to maintain political power over the political other. At the same time the ritual becomes the form of passage from the position of political other, enemy of the state, to a new entity—member of the Mukl community beyond the law. The violent rituals discussed in the context of Czechoslovak political prisoners were institutionalized. They were practiced within institutions such as prisons, the justice department, and work camps. Metaphorically, Jáchymov Hell, interrogation cells in the Bartolomějská Street police station, Pankrác prison, Bory and other prisons, and work camps located in Czechoslovakia are the spaces of death. I argue that the transformative experience of darkness in the context of political terror as a space of death is the transitional space through which the political other becomes a Mukl. The violence took place within the state-produced ritual. Such violent rituals were practiced to maintain the power of the state using physical and psychological torture, interrogations, trials, forced labor, post-prison personal harassment, and the constant threat of abduction, imprisonment or death. As I will show, the outcome of such a silencing ritual was, for many, alienation and exclusion from family, friends and the larger population.

In the past when presenting this project to non-Czech audiences, I have been often asked: How do Czechs define their identity? What is uniquely Czech about Muklhood? These have been challenging questions for me from both a professional and personal perspective. Because of my long residence in the United States, I can see, as an outsider, Czechs in a collective sense, caught in a geographic dilemma. By that I mean that the Czechs have a conflicted sense of belonging to Europe, well addressed by historian Jacques Rupnik. Rupnik discussed the Czech and Slovak sense of European identity, in the past and in the present. (For post-socialist belonging, see Rupnik 1995.)

My anthropological training and practice influence my careful approach to broad generalizations. While the Czech Republic is a small and relatively homogenous country, I am hesitant to rush to present the Czech national identity; however, as an insider, I am confident in emphasizing the role of national history in the self-consciousness of the Czech people. I agree with Ladislav Holy (Holy 1996) that Czechs define their identity based on their knowledge of historical and mythological processes in their country. These myths are reinforced from early childhood, built into the education system, and reproduced in various forms in adult life. Czech people have a strong sense of distinctive identity, but also desire to be connected to European identity and global identity. Individual experiences and values are shaped by belonging to a particular class, gender, political organization, religion, and family. Yet self, stereotype, and national tradition are part of a collective ethos.[11]

In this book I will demonstrate how public and private life, especially in the sphere of kinship and family, were reconfigured or transformed in the context of Mukls' subjectivity in the aftermath of political violence. In relation to the ideas about domestic and public space, I discuss the meaning of public face in contrast to private face in the Czech context. I refer to face not only as an actual place of revelation of individual histories, but also as a symbol of social invisibility and denial of human rights under the totalitarian political regime.

The ethnographic investigations of culturally specific forms of violence are illuminations of various modes of subjectivity formation. The production of violence in particular geographical locations is often perceived from the outside as a result of internal conflicts among ethnic, religious, or political groups. Current ethnographies of violence illustrate how local productions of violence are attached to larger political processes. Thus, some areas designated by the western world as violence prone are places of conflict, not because of the nature of violent ethnic groups, but because of the failure of local and global political structures to protect individuals within communities.

As I was working through the specifics, it became evident that for me to acquire an understanding of the formation of Czech Mukl subjectivities, it was necessary for me to see state terror as embodied in violent events, state rituals. I also needed to locate the memory of these events from the past into the present. Thus, I have been led to the decision to divide this book conceptually into two parts: Part I: Losing Face and Part II: Reconciliation.

Part I establishes the historical context, methodology, and the theoretical framework significant for this book. I introduce the concept of violent rituals as a major factor in the formation of Mukls' subjectivity and relatedness. Violent rituals are understood here as both forms of political practices developed under the institution of the totalitarian Czechoslovak Communist state and the passage to which selected citizens of the state were subjected. I conceptualize the Mukls' experience of violent rituals as passage through a dark space or the "space of death" in a process of defacement. I focus on the events of these passages: arrest, interrogation, and trial and investigate these events in relation to the ordinary, the notion of everyday, and to relatedness among kin and friends. I take the patterns of relatedness in Mukls' narratives and show how violent events changed their concepts of kinship and friendship.

In Part II, I discuss the Mukls' conditions today. My discussion is structured around specific events, and I read these events as rituals of Mukls' recovering their lost face. One of these events is an annual Mukl gathering, which takes place in the small town of Jáchymov, a place surrounded by former labor camps built to serve the uranium mines, where the regime used the Mukls as free labor during the 1950s. Within this framework of Mukl events, I discuss the meaning of their return to a place they call Jáchymov Hell. The Mukls' remembering in Jáchymov reveals their memories of the conditions in the camps. It shows their efforts to recover their voices by silent togetherness, and illuminates their hope invested in recovering justice under the current Czech judicial system. It is a labor of public exposure, of individual and collective memory, and it is the available archive.

Finally I conclude that the Mukls' annual gathering is a symbolic event signifying their recent desire to speak about their pain and betrayal, about their camaraderie, solidarity, and alternative family, but also about their alienation from Czech society and of the fragmentation of their community. The Mukls' have a strong desire to communicate their pain, and these memorial events have the potential to let them do that.

This study is an effort to tell their story based, as much as possible, on their own words, from the verbal and written texts they have produced. To protect my informants' privacy, I use only their first names. For the purposes of this book, I have asked my informants to sign a release to allow the use of their testimonies.

In 1948 Czechoslovakian political others were subjected to the state's produced violent practices of silencing, also known as a project of liquidation. Such practices in Czechoslovakia were modeled after Stalin's Soviet violent rituals (Arendt 1966), which originated in the Russian tsarist period (see Kennan 1958). What marks the difference between Czech political prisoners and political prisoners elsewhere is a particular violence developed during the Soviet totalitarian political system and practiced in Czechoslovakia. This was not random violence committed by the state government against its citizens, but rather a violent ritual organized, planned and institutionalized by the Soviet KGB and applied in Czechoslovakia by the Communist Party of Czechoslovakia. It was a passage intended to change or mute the political other. Arendt suggests that totalitarian violent practices are not only events or processes, they are also conditions to which people were subjected and under which they sought to survive. The institution of the Czechoslovak State used this strategic violence to maintain its power. Violent practices became essential for the ruling party's maintaining control in Communist societies between 1945 and 1989.

Over a long period during which state violence and terror affected not only Mukls and their families, but the whole society governed by the Czechoslovak Communist Party, the boundaries between specific violent events and everydayness collapsed. State terror, in its origins focused on the political enemy of the state, was diffused outside of institutions such as police, prisons and courts, the institutions guarding the state's political regimes, and became part of everyday life within the Czechoslovak state. Recovering the violence practiced by totalitarian political systems in Central and Eastern Europe fosters recovering from having lived through those violent events penetrating day-to-day life for over forty years.

NOTES

1. Czech historians, especially those who experienced Communist prisons, argued that organized anti-Communist resistance should be conceptualized as the third resistance. By resistance they mean an intentional fight and effort to overthrow the Communist regime during the period between 1948 and 1955 (see Babka and Weber 2002).

2. Knowing that Czech people are cautious about whom they invite into their homes for the first time, I did not ask at this stage if I could come to their homes. They were comfortable meeting me at my apartment. It helped that the apartment was in the city center, which was an area familiar to all.

3. This restaurant where Muklyněs held their monthly meetings was called Černý Pivovar (Black Brewery, which today is closed). They met the first Tuesday of each month. Mukls held a similar meeting the first Monday of the month. These were unofficial meetings held even during the Communist period, after their return from prison. The location of these meetings changed over time for reasons of safety. Mukls had open access to these gatherings in contrast to what later became meetings of the Confederation of Political Prisoners. Meetings had the character of informal gatherings and talks. I participated in several of them, and I was invited by Mukls to meet others.

4. It was the same apartment I had in 1995.

5. The Confederation of Political Prisoners (in Czech, Konfederace Politických Vězňů) was officially established after 1989, as a registered organization. The central office located in Prague was the primary location for the interviews I did in 1996 and 1997. For details on this organization see http:/protikomunisticke.misto.cz/panel. html.

6. The average interview lasted from one to two hours; some follow-up interviews were two to three hours.

7. The Milada Horáková Club was established in memory of Horáková, who was one of the political actors persecuted in the spring of 1948. Many members of this club are Mukls and former academics. I visited the location where the club meets regularly, and I was invited to one of the meetings and introduced to some members whom I later interviewed. It was through this club that I was informed about a number of Mukls' biographies. One of the members, Milan Nevole, is a publisher focused on publishing Mukls' memoirs.

8. Individual Mukls I worked with who are not living in Prague: Doctor K., a Mukl's wife, and a Muklyně, who are not quoted directly but are important informants in the process.

9. The Soviet Army invasion of August 21, 1968, was intended to suppress the developing political and social independence of Czechoslovakia from the Soviet Union. Russian and other Warsaw Pact nations' tanks entered Prague. The violent confrontation between Soviet soldiers and Czech citizens became a significant historical moment dividing the period of Stalinist Socialism and *Normalizace* (Normalization) in Czechoslovakia (see Pithart 1990). Normalization refers to the time period between 1968 and 1989, when the Communist Party reestablished its political control. From Mukls' perspective, living conditions under Normalization reflected different political and civic experiences than those of the 1950s.

10. Social trauma and the remaking of everyday life is the subject of essays edited by Veena Das, Arthur Kleinman, Margaret Lock, Mamphela Ramphele, and Pamela Reynolds in the publication *Remaking a World* (2001). In 1993 the editors planned a series of volumes to examine anthropological questions about relationships between and among victims of violence, involving state and local communities and individuals. In the volume *Remaking a World*, the ethnographic focus is on case studies that emphasize reconciliation, understood as coming to terms with the past. Two previous volumes, *Social Suffering* (Das, Kleinman, and Lock 1997) and *Violence and Subjectivity* (Das, Kleinman, Ramphele, and Reynolds 2000) are investigations of the different ways in which social force inflicts harm on individuals and collectivities.

11. For more on Czech identity, nation and myth see *The Little Czech and the Great Czech Nation* by Ladislav Holy (Holy 1990).

Chapter Two

Arrest

ARREST AND KINSHIP

Čeněk was very proud of the view from the balcony. His balcony on the rooftop of a Prague center city apartment building was almost bigger than the attached apartment.

In 1996, during the second year of my fieldwork in Prague, I was invited one evening to Čeněk's place for a visit. It was my first time in his small studio apartment which used to be his mother's place. Our plan was to talk about his production of a radio show in the briefly liberalized 1960s about prisons, camps and Muklhood during the 1950s era.

I could see Prague's red rooftops, church towers, and Prague castle in the distance. Immediately below was the dark, small courtyard of the infamous Bartolomějská Street police station. When looking down to the police station, the courtyard looked insignificant, just like any other typical Prague courtyard. Čeněk saw me looking down and said, "That's where they took me when I was arrested for the first time. This used to be my mother's apartment. They were taking me in wearing handcuffs and I looked up. There on the balcony stood my mother. It was the last time I saw her. After that I never saw her again. She died when I was in prison."

In this section I want to show how, for Mukls, the event of arrest by the totalitarian state police was a significant rupture in their belonging to family and state. I do this based on direct links and types of linguistic sequences that Mukls made. I also suggest that consideration of and examination of the event of arrest will allow us to see how one's sense of self during the arrest, and lasting images of it, are significant points of reference within Mukls' remembering. This remembering illuminates the potential for arrest to reach beyond the boundaries of time and space and become part of everyday life for all Mukls'.

The narratives that follow are based on two types of ethnographic data collected in the summers of 1995 and 1996. The first text comes from the transcript of my visit with Čeněk in his Prague home in 1995. The second texts are transcriptions of individual Mukls' narratives which signify the moment of change, the rupture, the moment of no longer belonging to family and nation. Some of these narratives I recorded at the Mukl Party headquarters in Prague, which is located in a building belonging today to the Czech police. Others were recorded at my rented apartment on Bartolomějská Street, the street on which the infamous police station which specialized in interrogations is located. Mukls' memories were full of loss, alienation and pain, yet in their faces there was hope for reconciliation.

Čeněk's memory, knowledge accessible through his speech, is the alternative available archive. I realized that the memory of this event, constructed through the retelling of narratives, becomes the "figure of speech" (Amin 1995). The short episode cited above from our, Čeněk's and my, time on the balcony became for me a critical moment for understanding the rupture in his kinship bond by a violent event—arrest. It is the memory of this event which was "folded into everyday life" (Das and Poole 2004).

The view which he experienced during his arrest is today part of his everyday landscape. Violence merged into visibility, and visibility creates violence constituted in the present. Today, many years after his arrest, Čeněk is still caught in the power of the "scopic regime" (Feldman 2001). By living above the police station he has to face what Veena Das defined as the "everyday work of repair" (Das 2000:208). From our conversation, I could see how this labor of repair triggers other memories—the memory of the passage through the space of death, interrogations, torture, trial, the death sentence changed to a life sentence, the life in prisons and camps, and controlled freedom—all characteristic of post-prison life. Čeněk emphasized that the most painful of all was his memory of the last moment he saw his mother alive, a painful vision impossible to overcome.

Langer addresses the difficulty of constructing new narratives about evil from survivors' testimonies. "Once we enter the tentative world of duration, leaving behind the security of chronology, we realize that life after atrocity is not a call to new unity but only a form of private and communal endurance, based on mutual toleration rather than mutual love" (Langer 1997:63). To survive trauma is not to heal but to endure, and the previous experience can not be undone by the next (Langer 1991:56).

While the details of Čeněk's arrest are unique, his arrest is also symbolic of the rupture of kinship ties marked by violence for all Mukls. After their arrest many political prisoners were taken to Pankrác police station for interrogations. Some remembered their trips on the bus with dark windows, which took them from the prison cell to Bartolomějská station in the center of Prague. Those Mukls were invisible to other Czechs and yet, they, the prisoners, could see life outside. Memories of these transports were marked by powerless feelings and desires to scream for help, the same desires people had when taken to concentration camps during the Nazi occupation. When talking about arrest, many Mukls, like Čeněk, spoke about the loss of their relatives, their homes and work. Memory of these events is deeply rooted and is one of the patterns in Mukls' speech.

Dagmar Šimková, Muklyně, wrote about her arrest:

> So goodbye, and I turned one more time to my mum. As we (I and the agents) walked down the steps in our garden, I turned one more time to see the terrace. It was there my mother always stayed when I was going out. On the shoulders of angels in the garden were more and more leaves. "Take a careful look, you reactionary whore. You will never come back as long you live," said one of the StB agents to me. And he was right! (Šimková 1994)

Under the Communist regime in Czechoslovakia, family and home had the potential to offer its members solidarity against the political opposition—the state. With an awareness of this potential, the state targeted the family. Many partners, parents, or children became alienated. Olga, one of the youngest women among the arrested, told me about the arrest of her entire family and her reunion with her mother in prison after months of isolation and not knowing her parents' circumstances before the trial. During our talk she would often return to the issue of her family's being separated. When she returned from prison she was allowed to live with her mother. Even when her father returned and they could live together again, Olga's family never recovered from the separation. Olga remembered in just a few sentences, but very directly, the change in her parents' relationship after they reconnected. "My parents were also arrested. They arrested the whole family. My mother and I returned first and then Father. They changed, people changed in prison. The prison alienated them from each other. They divorced."

Hilda spoke about her arrest through the loss of bonds with her husband.

> I had a husband, he was a dentist, and when they arrested me, he immediately divorced me and then remarried again. The guard brought me a piece of paper to sign—a divorce paper. Thank God, my parents had a nanny, Mařinka, who took care of my son. She took care of all my family when I was in the prison.

Alienation between Mukls and family members after arrest and imprisonment was inevitable. Children, whose parents were in prison, had to adjust quickly to their new situations. Martin, the son of Milu, who was arrested and interrogated for eight months, spoke about his childhood and living through the arrest and imprisonment of his mother.

As a child I knew something out of the ordinary was going on when two men came, our maid woke up my mother from her afternoon nap, and then two men took her away. I was looking from the window, they walked her between them and so they seated her in the back of the car. Then I didn't see her for fourteen months. We knew it was not unusual; all my friend's parents were in prison.

I was allowed to send one postcard a month. The postcard was my aunt's decision—since they opened the letters anyway. I never got anything from her in the prison. At the time of my mother's arrest she and my father were divorced and I went to live with him for the summer. After that my father made the decision to send me to boarding school. In this school were not just children of prisoners but also the sons of Czech diplomats living abroad. She returned in the summer. I was with my father and didn't want to leave my playing behind to go see her. My father convinced me to go. Of course I missed her, but I was just a boy who wanted also to play. Then I traveled across Czech by myself on the train to Letovice, where my great aunt had a summerhouse, and there I was supposed to spend a week or two with my mother.

In a later conversation Martin reflected on what he called "the amazing malleability and adaptability of a child."

My mother was taken away from me when I was eleven. Given that drastic, traumatic experience, I didn't suffer that much. I adapted to the new reality of motherless life very quickly. Yes, there was a tear here and there, like when there was no mama at Christmas, but on the whole, I was not traumatized, I went on with my life, or so I thought. The full impact on my development of the fact that at the very impressionable age of eleven or twelve, I was left without day-to-day parental guidance, is something that came to me much later, when I was in my late thirties or forties. Only then did I realize how the natural development of my moral fiber and spiritual values was interrupted by my becoming completely independent much too early and how long it took me to reconnect to what was interrupted.

Martin and many other children of prisoners had to adapt and go on. Yet, while working through their narratives, many like him had to negotiate the rupture of their ordinary lives, the disappearance of their parents that was hard to understand, the loss of everyday contact or the redefining of relationships when parents returned. The early experience of independence was not without knowing solitude and alienation.

Fatherhood was equally affected by state terror. In Mukls' testimonies there is no difference, based on gender divisions, in the amount and frequency of remembered parenthood. A number of men testified that arrest interrupted their lives when they had just gotten married or were expecting their first child. Čeněk, Rudolf and František were such fathers.

Čeněk: When I was arrested I was married and had a year old daughter, who I saw following my release when she was 11 years old. My father lost his job and had to go work on building a dam. My wife lost her job. She was strong, she waited for me all those years. My daughter couldn't go to school (by that, Čeněk meant higher education), even when I returned home in the sixties. The visits in the prison were allowed once every three months for ten minutes. They only allowed two people to visit. My wife came with my mother. It was a harsh rupture of our environment and a reconnection with the past.

Rudolf: After I was arrested it was hard. My wife was pregnant and my son was born six months after my arrest. Visits were allowed infrequently. During these I could hardly get to know my son. We began to live together when he was eleven years old. Only then could I fully parent him. It was hard for him to get to high school even though he was a good student. In the end we managed to get him to the university, but he was kicked out soon. He emigrated to Hamburg and thanks to his talent and strong will he studied in the university and today he is in a good position, even though he is not a Czech citizen, but German.

František: Before I was arrested I got married and during my arrest my wife was pregnant. Our son was born when I was in the prison. I saw him for the first time when he was two, several times through the prison bars. We met when he was eleven years old. When I returned from prison my son said to me: "Daddy would you come to meet me at the school tomorrow, so that the other children can see I also have a daddy?" I was called to the school and told that he cannot continue his schooling after elementary; he is the son of a prisoner and therefore he can't be part of the intelligentsia. Later on the teacher called me to school and asked if we attended church. I was angry and finally said that I am the parent and he comes with me and that is the bottom line. In the end my son was interested in philosophical studies, but that was out of the question, so he went to study agriculture.

From these examples we can see how Mukls' parental connectedness was impacted by the state. When Mukls spoke about the ruptures of family relatedness, the sound of their voices carried the pain from the past. The pain of the memory of loss is not overcome by the life they lived afterwards. Fatherhood and motherhood were relationships through which many Mukls suffered pain. Pain impacted those parents who were denied contact with their children on two levels: alienation from their children and then later when their children had difficulty in getting higher education and jobs because of their parents' identification as Mukls. The state used kinship relations as a means of control and punishment. Many relationships did not survive the systematic attempts by the state to rupture family relatedness.

The interruption of family life under the totalitarian political regime is re-membered by Mukls as a very specific event, such as Čeněk's remembering, but also as a long-term struggle of missing their relatives and being marked as enemies. For many, like Čeněk, it was the loss of relatives who died before their return. Over a long period of time, many lost closeness to their children or partners. From a Mukl's point of view, arrest was the first moment of his isolation from *rodina*, family; it was the painful loss of the possibility of everyday kinship relatedness and the loss of his comfort zone.

The intentional disruption of domestic life, "the ground of all making" (Reynolds 2000:141) as Reynolds put it when reporting on family related-ness under the violence in South Africa, is critical for subjectivity formation. Reynolds showed in her investigations of families exposed to violence that if kinship is exposed to extreme stress, existing conventions that hold vari-ous categories together are forced apart (Reynolds 2000:141). In the Czech context, between 1948 and 1989, *rodina*, family, provided its members with a gift of a space. In contrast to public space, this private space had the potential to offer not only freedom of speech and political solidarity but also emotional comfort. It was a comfort zone, a place for emotional rest from the constant experience of *nedůvěry* (mistrust), *lži* (lies) and *zrady* (betrayal) so character-istic for public space in Czechoslovakia.

PRISON OUTSIDE OF THE PRISON

The disruption of family relatedness by the state produced violence and pain in individuals' lives. The intentional destruction of family ties affected not just Mukls, but their parents, spouses, children and other relatives. The denial of parent and child relationships went in two directions: through arrest a Mukl or Muklyně lost his or her place as a parent, the child lost his connection to his parent, and the parents of Mukls lost their connections to their children. Families suffered along with the prisoners. After a political other's arrest, the family he left behind was moved out of their home to a smaller place or relo-cated to a different city or region. Many Mukls talked about forced relocation.

Mulkyně Květa spoke about loss of domestic space. "My mother didn't know about me for two years, she was left behind alone in the four-bedroom apartment and so they moved her right away to a small apartment in Nusle." Otta, one of the Mukls, related details of his arrest.

I was twenty-two-years-old when I was arrested. For my parents it was psycho-logically difficult. On the street their friends crossed to the other sidewalk. The state police under the command of an officer that I knew from the war harassed my father. They visited him repeatedly with a written statement to sign stating that he disowns me as a son, because I am an anti-state element. Once they took my father to the forest, tied him up with rope and then placed him on the train tracks, and said in ten minutes the express train is coming and he needs to sign the paper, if not they will leave him there. They pulled him away just as the train was coming. The next week they came again. This time they hung him by a rope and when he was suffocating they cut him down. He experienced this for a quarter of a year. In his job he lost his position and was given a lower level job. My father died one year before I returned. My mother collapsed psychologically. She was in the psychiatric hospital twice. I want to say that they marked our families and no one speaks about that a lot. I did what I did to myself, but why did my parents have to suffer for me?

In our conversation Otta emphasized his discomfort about the silence surrounding the suffering of Mukls' relatives. "Nobody speaks about the suffering of their family. Everybody speaks about their own pain, but what about our families? We were young, strong, but our parents suffered for many years."

Members of the families of political others were only permitted to work in jobs which were highly physical ones, often night shifts, and in jobs where they could not come into contact with the rest of the population. Occupations which allowed intellectual involvement or social interaction were prohibited to members of prisoners' families. They were enemies of the regime. The children of prisoners were not permitted to enter high school or university. They were stigmatized as children of individuals who were dangerous and harmful to the regime. Family relations became an additional means of psychological torture and a useful tool to feed the prisoners' fears for their loved ones. The sudden denial of parenting immediately after arrest, one of the most painful punishments, became one of the fundamental elements of both Mukls' suffering in the camps and of the family members who were left behind. Families were often relocated; they lost their home, property, land, and jobs, and were continuously harassed by the state police. Alienation from society was for the Mukls' families another form of prison. The totalitarian state punished its citizens through their kinship ties. Belonging to the family of a political other became, under the Communist regime, a reason for exclusion from society. One Mukl's wife who was left behind remembered:

My husband knew what was happening, people were arrested. One morning he came to our boys' room and played with them; he got up one hour early so that he could spend time with them and then left for work. That day he didn't come home from work. Three men came and looked through everything and then they took his things. I didn't see him until one year after that day.

My husband got twenty-two years. He was given a 10,000 crown fine to pay. One evening, late, nine thirty, a policeman with a dog came by. I was shaking

from not knowing what would happen. He came to tell me that they had transported my husband to the heavy prison. For three years I lived on people's charity,
I couldn't find work. They moved us out of our apartment. When I tried to get
work as a cleaning lady, I was called in front of the committee. Groups of guys
were sitting around the table and I was given a chair opposite them. They told me
I couldn't have a job because I would have access to all the offices and that is not
acceptable. I begged them that I have to feed my children, but nothing happened.
I collapsed psychologically. I was alone to raise my sons. I was in contact with
another wife of a Mukl who was in the same prison as my husband. She and I
became close friends and shared everything.

When my husband returned it took us two years to get used to each other. He
came with all kinds of habits that I had to accept. He was often explosive over
things in the way that he hadn't been before. He also had a deteriorated nervous
system, just like me.

From this Mukl's wife's narratives, we can read that while Mukls were
arrested, their relatives experienced another form of prison, the prison of
invisible walls and wires, in which exclusion took a different form than the
real prison. For the Mukls' relatives, the Czechoslovakian State, under the
Communist regime, created a new type of prison, walls and barriers of harassment, ignominy and separation from family and society. This was the life of
Mukl's kin, life within the state's iron borders, and a life for all behind the
Iron Curtain.

I intend to show how kinship ties in Czechoslovakia were not only lost but
transformed during the totalitarian regime. Alienation or loss in the prisoners'
relationships was followed by the formation of new friendships, new families.
These changes are deeply encoded in Mukls' subjectivity.

ARREST AND THE TEMPORALITY OF CITIZENSHIP

Arrest is also remembered by Mukls as a state counter-event to the radical
movement they organized against the Communist government. After the end
of the Nazi occupation, their fear of becoming citizens of a Soviet colony in
Central Europe led them to the act they defined in their narratives as one of
moral and ethical duty to protect the homeland, *vlast*, from Sovietization.

During the second year of my fieldwork I made a connection with the
Mukls' organization—the Confederation of Political Prisoners. There I met
other Mukls and Muklynès and among them a medical doctor, Jiří K. As a
young man Jiří fought with the partisans against the Nazi army occupying
Czechoslovakia, and when the war was over he got involved in the movement opposing the emerging Communist dictatorship. He was arrested, his
family lost their private property to the state and Jiří was sent to the camps.

What makes his testimony different from other Mukls is his position in the camps where he was forced to practice medicine. This ranged from small interventions, which kept the Mukls alive in between interrogations, to complicated operations done in a highly improvised manner in the absence of any medical equipment. Given his position, Jiří was often an intermediary between Mukls and the camp or prison establishment. When speaking about his experience, he made many connections to the overall political discourse, which highlighted ideas emerging in others' narratives. This is how Jiří began his narrative:

> In 1949 I was mugged by a group of *estébaku* (StB-Secret Police) and shipped off to the prison. The reason was that a number of people couldn't look at what the Communist party was doing in this beautiful country called Czech and Moravia. We formed illegal groups, which tried to defend it. It was a foolish idea, because we should have all known that it was directed from the Soviet Union, with the help of the KGB, and perhaps we knew, but overlooked it. So it was lost in advance. We reacted radically and patriotically and, as a result, less carefully, which caused the situation for us when we were arrested.

The strong sense of belonging to homeland and consciousness of one's obligation of the moral and ethical duty to protect this place of belonging was, in 1945, already sensitized by the Czechoslovakian experience of Nazi occupation. Former freedom fighters, among them Mukls, who fought against the Nazi occupation of *Čech* (Bohemia) and Moravia were apprehensive about the undetermined future of Czechoslovakia. The motherland became a symbol of one's right to civic freedom within a post-1945, and recently divided, Central Europe.

Rudolf, a professional soldier, whom I also met in the Confederation, described his actions.

> In 1939, when Germany occupied *Čech* and Moravia, I, of course, as a patriot, *vlastenec*, and a person who gave a promise to our Republic to protect our freedom and independence under the Army oath, decided not to serve the Germans. I fought in the Czech Army from abroad. When 1948 came, I of course, couldn't agree with what was happening, because we knew that we fought the Germans for freedom and independence.

Mukls, acting upon this strong sense of belonging, soon found themselves in the position of political other in relation to the political interests of the Soviets and those of their domestic sympathizers. These interconnected notions of citizenship, belonging, ethics, and morals became central to the political power struggle between 1945 and 1948. One of the first Muklyněs I interviewed, Jitka M., openly expressed this strong sense of her citizenship and

duty to protect her country. "I was active in a group. I decided consciously for
resistance towards the totality. I am from a strongly anti-Communist family,
so I had this resistance inside me."

Many Mukls described active involvement in the antigovernment movement as the cause of arrest in similar ways. Albína: "I was teaching at the
University. Around '48–'49 my students were active and when they were
seriously threatened with arrest I helped them to get out of the country. This
was the reason that I was given fifteen years in prison." Vojta K. explains
that, "after February '48 I began my illegal activity. I organized crossings
over the border for students, politicians, and intellectuals. This activity continued until 1949, when I was arrested." Olga V. recalls that "my parents
owned a pension in a spa city, not far from the border. After the Communists came to power, my parents got involved in organized anti-Communist
activities. They were helping people over the border. I was nineteen years
old at the time and not involved. They arrested the whole family and confiscated our property."

The state's justification for the arrest of the political other was based
on its understanding, or construct, of the Mukls' betrayal of the Peoples'
Republic. This accusation allowed the state to legalize acts of marking and
liquidating the political other. Arrest was legitimized by new laws. In 1948
Czechoslovak political others were silenced under the judicial system. The
formulation of new laws served as both justification and means for the totalitarian regime's liquidation of political others. The courtrooms became places
arranged for performances of the criminalization of suspected enemies of the
republic who were seen as criminal traitors and dangerous to the implementa-
tion of Communist ideals.

Paradoxically, for Mukls, it was their consciousness of citizenship which
empowered them to act against totalitarian political power. Yet betrayal of
citizenship was the state's reason for Mukls' arrests. In Mukls' arrests we can
see how the nation-state betrayed its citizens by accusing them of nation-state
betrayal. Close examination of an event such as arrest reveals the instability
or temporality of citizenship. The specific modes of suffering in the context
of transnational discourse, seen as caused by displacement of one's sense
of belonging to the nation and further production of alienation, is a central
theme of Daniel's ethnography of Sri Lankan Tamil refugees (Daniel 1996).
Daniel's interpretation of various types of suffering shows how one's sense of
belonging to a nation is connected to one's own construction of subjectivity.
Daniel pointed out a moment of change within the realm of citizenship for
Sri Lankan Tamil refugees in England. The refugees were caught between
the nation-state's failure to fulfill the promise implicit in Sri Lankan citizenship and the healing mission they sought in England. As Daniel put it: "The

nation-state promised to restore to the chords of collective discontent in attunement with collective consciousness, to recover for its people a moral order where there is only disorder, and to return its nationals to the path of their intended destiny" (Daniel 1997:309). Mukls' arrests were events during which there occurred what Daniel defined as a "deliberation," a "moment of habit change" (Daniel 1997:322). In the Mukls' context, the political other's habit, the patterns of feeling, action, and thought of belonging to the homeland, disappeared rapidly through the event of arrest.

BELONGING TO THE NATION

Czechoslovakia's political belonging to Europe has historically been tension-filled for the Czech and the Slovak peoples. The unification of the Czech and Slovak peoples within one state, Czechoslovakia, in 1918 was an act of emancipation from the Austro-Hungarian Empire after its fall in 1917. The period of building and establishing a new modern state is known as the First Republic (see Táborský 1970; for a historical outline, see Fawn 2000). The First Republic is significant as a historical marker in the history of the Czech and Slovak nations, remembered as the moment of emergence for a modern democratic state with national independence and identity. National identity was constructed based on opposition to the Germans, Austrians and Hungarians with whom Czechs and Slovaks had shared political and economic space under the Austro-Hungarian Empire.

The process of building a modern Czechoslovakian state was interrupted by the Nazi occupation in 1938. The liberation from Nazi Germany in 1945 was followed by a new, silent occupation of Czechoslovakia by the Soviet Union. During and immediately after World War II, many Czechoslovak citizens were not ready to passively accept the Soviet model of political power and were actively involved in anti-Communist and anti-Soviet resistance.

In the post–World War II period (1945–1948), the Czechoslovakian political and social order was destabilized by the presence of the Soviet Army and the threat of Sovietization. Based on his own experience, Jaroslav Brodský expressed his view of the post-liberation atmosphere in his book *Solution Gamma* (Brodský 1971). He wrote,

> It was a strange month of May. Church bells sounded the victory, while beneath them; the army was stealing the monstrances from the altars. Like evil shadows, officers of the intelligence service were moving about the town in dusty uniforms, side by side with former informers, pointing fingers.

Wherever they went, soldiers kissed little children and raped their mothers.
(Brodský 1971:11)

Brodský indicates that along with the feeling of joy surrounding the end of
World War II, there also existed the fear of impending arrest. "That night we
watched out of the window; the soldiers had dispersed already, and a neigh-
bor lady came over to tell us that a lot of people had been arrested, that some
kind of committee was doing it, but that it might not be the right one, because
two of its members were former Gestapo informers" (Brodský 1971). These
new formations of power caused new sociopolitical tensions that led to major
conflicts in Czechoslovakia between 1945 and 1948 (see Feierabend 1988;
Hejl and Kaplan 1986; Táborský 1970; Tigrid 1982). The radical Communist
Revolution in February 1948 in Czechoslovakia resulted from two post–
World War II developments: a Soviet political project[1] in Central Europe and
internal political conflict in Czechoslovakia.

Mukls spoke about historical continuity in Czechoslovakia. The 1945
liberation from Nazi Germany, based on Mukls' testimonies, led directly to
a new silent occupation of Czechoslovakia by the Soviet Union. As Edward
Táborský put it: "Having just survived the horror of domination by a dictatorship of the extreme right, the Czech and Slovaks found themselves face to
face with the dire menace of the dictatorship of the extreme left" (Táborský
1970). The forced return of German minorities to Germany, the emigration
of the surviving Jewish population to Israel and elsewhere, and the chaos
associated with remaking life after the war all contributed to widespread
disorder. The nation-state held the promise of comforting its citizens during
this time of political tensions deriving from newly formed Central European
political geographies, yet it failed its citizens, some to the extreme of actual
or attempted liquidation.

CONCLUSION

The 1948 arrests sharpened the political divisions in Czechoslovakia. From
the political elites' point of view, arrest was an "activity of policing" (Asad
1997:289) within the institution of a modern state. For the state, arrest "is to
be understood as a practical logic integral to the maintenance of the nation-
state sovereignty, much like warfare" (Asad 1997:296). From the Mukls'
point of view, the political project of intensive silencing of political others is
tied to arrest and that marks the beginning of being forced to live a political
fiction. Many testimonies signal Mukls' confrontation with death. For me,
it is a rich point of reference for the Mukls' early formations of their own
subjectivities. The function of arrest, "a biographical experience capable of

generating collective political meanings" (Feldman 2000: 97), surrounded as it was by silence and secrecy, was to generate collective violence and political subjectivity. The arrests were "the political art of individualizing disorder" (Feldman 2001). But most important, the arrests were a passageway to violent death, the making of a Mukl, or the "corridor that opens up paramilitary praxis to a self-reflexive framing power, agency, and the body" (Feldman 2000:106).

The arrest was the moment of habit change, the deliberate disruption of two targeted institutions—kinship and citizenship. Kinship and citizenship ties, relatedness and belonging, which were selected for destruction under the totalitarian regime, became instrumental in the process of liquidation. The state's denial of kinship and citizenship became a powerful strategy within the long-term political project of liquidation, practiced as a violent ritual. When Mukls remember arrest, they link the loss of kinship and citizenship to a moral voice calling out against evil. Such speech provides insight into the very core of Mukls' ideas. It is just that moral register in their voice which underlies the ways in which they define their positions.

Pamela Reynolds's investigation of the effects of state violence on families in South Africa is an excellent example of the necessity for new forms of reception and models for analysis of the effects of violence. Just as the South African government targeted family units to disrupt individual ties, the Czechoslovak Communist government aimed to gain power over its citizens through the strategic fragmentation of the family.

The subject of kinship proved to be central to many Mukls' testimonies. In my narratives I will consistently re-examine the role of relatedness, namely kinship, exposed to different forms of violence.

The loss of personal attachments and freedom, as linked to moral political choices, is an extremely important pattern in the Mukls' ways of making sense of their own lives. The Mukls' view of the Communist regime was framed by the violent character of political power defined, on one level, by organized violent acts against the citizens of the state in the name of an ideology. It was framed too by practices adapted from the Soviet political power in place in Czechoslovakia. In Mukls' eyes the state and its agents failed to promote "good" and therefore lost the capacity to practice moral politics. By this they mean that it was the state and its agents which intentionally inflicted pain and evil on a Mukl and his/her family. That violated human spaces and led to events that should not have happened. In the Mukls' view the state and its actors were responsible for putting its victims' humanity in jeopardy through harmful events that resulted in life long tragedies for many. In their consciousness Mukls' identity is synonymous with rebellion against the evils of political fiction.[2] Today, after the fall of the Communist regime in Czechoslovakia, Mukls are reclaiming their lost citizenship and maintaining strong bonds with their new family. (I will discuss Mukls' forms of recent claims for their new family in Part II.) Their politics are tied to an effort to reconstruct their history of suffering and to speak in the voice which was intended to be silenced; through these strategies of reconciliation, they see possibilities to gain back some of what they lost. The family life they lost cannot be reclaimed. Their relatives died or left them, while over the years they worked on overcoming the mutual alienation caused by separation.

In this chapter I have shown how the event of arrest has been established by Mukls as an early point of reference for defining their subjectivity. My intention was to emphasize the contrast between an individual Mukl's point of view and the type of political power imposed on all of them. Concerned with narratives of conditions under such imposed political violence, I sought to recover their voice.[3] I have discussed two types of Mukls' belonging, belonging to family and belonging to state. Mukls' kinship and citizenship belonging was dramatically affected by their active resistance or passive disbelief in the new Communist regime. It was a type of relatedness through which the politically powerful tried to control and punish the political other. A Mukl's arrest represents for him an early moment of transition in kinship ties marked by the state. The transformation of relations in the context of state and family, occurring after arrest, became one of the major aspects of social changes under the totalitarian political system in Czechoslovakia.

I have emphasized the relationship between individual and communal experience, not as mutually exclusive, but interactive. What Mukls share is passage through violent rituals, but the consequences and individual responses vary. To understand Mukls' discourse it is essential to recognize their shared and stated perception of arrest as a violent act. Mukls in the organized political resistance movement expected to be arrested, but for many others, arrest was unanticipated, a mistake, an act of disappearance (London 1968:26) that changed their lives. I will return to the subject of kinship and citizenship later in my discussion of torture and pain, and also in the context of individual Mukls' alternative forms of belonging in the face of state-imposed denial of contact with family members and civic membership.

NOTES

1. By Soviet political project I mean the 1945 Soviet political expansion into Central Europe after World War II (see Feierabend 1988, Kaplan 1989, Lesák 2000, Táborský 1970).

2. For this context see works of Václav Havel on the concepts of truth and political discourse (Havel 1989, Havel 1995).

3. For more on subaltern voice see Guha 1997.

Chapter Three

Interrogations

Arrest and interrogation, like other forms of terror, transform social life and historical experience into a political rite of passage.

—Feldman (2001:142)

THE TORTURE DILEMMA

Arrested men and women spent months in prison before they were called to trial. During their imprisonment they were subjected to continuous interrogations. Even a suspicion of anti-state actions became sufficient reason for arrest and interrogation. Mukls testify that they were forced to admit having engaged in activities against the state. Torture became a routine part of the interrogations. Interrogation, understood as irrational and brutal episodes, is unproductive in terms of its goals of retrieving information, and it is the starting point for narratives of survival.

In this chapter, I intend to show various modes of subjectivity during the interrogations and look at the journey Mukls were forced to take through the space of death. I present Mukls' torture narratives as one type of evidence. I perceive the examination of interrogations as central to an experiential understanding of Czech Mukls. This evidence is critical to an understanding of how, when they remember it, Mukls themselves make sense out of their suffering. I also will demonstrate how interrogation rituals embodied the "verification and rationalization of the produced power" (Feldman 2001:120), even fictionalized power, and how simulation of death is accomplished through concepts of time, space and vision. I present the StB archive, closely tied to the interrogations, as a materialized location for political power. Finally

I seek to show how, in spite of Mukls' feelings of their dehumanization and degradation by the interrogators, some moments of interrogation actually produced, through the Mukls' internal voices, the experience of relatedness, seen across the boundaries of time and space.

Today, after years of contact, we, Mukls and I, do not talk about the torture they experienced. They know that I know. We share the knowledge of their pain caused by torture, locked in our silence. But we also now share an ambivalent dilemma of torture narratives. We are caught between two paradigms: disbelief in claims of victimhood and a desire to tell the story, a desire to be understood and to reconcile. Pain in the context of violence is, as Das suggests, "a spiritual as well as intellectual problem" (Das 1997).

Mukls do not like to identify themselves as victims, but at the same time their pain from torture is deeply embedded in their memories. They face the difficulty of communicating the severity of their suffering; they struggle to find the grammar to relate the torture narratives, which are a necessity for healing. And because healing from violent trauma is "a kind of relationship with death" (Das 1997:78), pain, language and body are an inevitable triangle. As the Mukls conceptualize and come to terms with the violence they suffered, they construct their subjectivity.

During our recorded interviews, the moment we reached the subject of the torture they experienced, many Mukls became emotionally distressed. The memory of interrogations caused pain. Some cried; others remained silent. Sometimes the pain overshadowed the voice. From the early stages of my research, I have been uncomfortable asking Mukls about the particular torture practices they endured. Yet many broke the silence; many, especially women, spoke about the torture in microscopic detail. They spoke about isolation, humiliation and degradation produced by physical and psychological pain. The prisoners, who were stripped of any rights during interrogations, found themselves in the space that Agamben called a "bare life" (Agamben 2000).

Mukls' memories of trauma become a memory of humiliation, presented to me in the light of the pain of others. In their memory of the humiliation of others, Mukls suggested that there is a difference between men and women's experiences of pain. Their memory of gendered pain is connected to a concept of a "gender division of labor over pain" (Das 1997 and Ross 2003).

The temporal space and violence within the act of interrogation allowed me to see how violence was worked into the power of the regime. The boundaries among real violence and imaginary violence and terror were diffused by various spaces assigned to particular acts of violence. Prison space is, in the Foucaultian sense, the architecture of discipline that rationalizes the offender, an action upon an active body, a sensorium of the body; "the power is formed through the formation of the senses" (Feldman 1991:123).

In the previous chapter, I emphasized arrest as a significant event for the early formation of Mukls' subjectivity. My analysis in this chapter depends only on interrogation narratives of Mukls or their family members. Recorded speech or written testimony, based on Mukls' remembering, is treated as an ethnographic archive, in which the text reveals multiple registers. My approach is based on a linguistic methodology of textual analysis, in particular Bakhtin's concept of double register within language discourse (Bakhtin 1996).

While trying to convey the urgency of bringing Mukls' stories to public light I share with Mukls their discomfort when speaking of torture. At the same time, I am also aware of the power embodied in the torture narratives. My own hesitance and dilemma in constructing the narratives of torture are based on my determination to avoid limiting the category of torture to "the application of physical pain" (Asad 1997:297). Mukls' narratives reflect, for example, the pain from loss and the co-suffering of family members, in particular, the loss of parenting or the rupture in marital bonds. These family relations became a resource that the state police, the StB, and its employees, torturers, and prison guards, could use as a means of inflicting pain. This type of torture and punishment took very specific forms: disappearance, denial of contact with family from the time of arrest, denial of information about the arrested person, withholding information about the prisoner's family, house searches, threats during interrogations, and psychological blackmail. But many reflect and remember relatedness as a mechanism of survival. I learned that Mukls negotiated their pain through the means of this relatedness. Family relations at the time of imprisonment meant, for prisoners, a connection with the past, but also became a hope for the future.

Talal Asad reminds us that from the modern state's point of view the use of torture needs to be understood as a practical logic, "integral to the maintenance of the national state's sovereignty, much like warfare" (Asad 1997:296). The thoroughly interrogated prisoner was ready, in the state's eyes, for trial. For the state, interrogations were conducted to transform the political other and provide "the foundation for the rationalization of power and thus the fictionalization of its violence" (Feldman 2001:115). For a Mukl, interrogation became the principal stage in a rite of passage, leading towards the making of a Mukl.

Continuous interrogations preparing the prisoner for trial were the state prescribed methods of making a prisoner confess, thereby approving and participating in the political fiction constructed by the state. A fundamental aspect of this passage was the removal of time. Feldman conceptualized this as a simulation of death that is achieved through darkness, silence, and immobility, the "techniques of petrification" (Feldman 1991:137).

Torture does not apply power; rather, it manufactures it from the raw ingredient of the captive body. Interrogation, like arrest, is embodied significantly in the rites of political passage. What makes interrogation a rite of passage is the simulation of death, the restoration of time, and the "transformational movement of the political actor through the interior of the state" (Feldman 2000:142). Time is also removed as a cognitive reference. The real time of the prisoner is manipulated through the wall clock, the lost sense of day and night during the interrogations, and other distortions. This disorder of time is linked to instrumental torture as the interrogator seeks to generate truth.

In the case of Mukls, absolute invisibility to society and very limited visibility to family over long periods of time meant loss of social face. Both Taussig's and Feldman's understanding of the interrelatedness between the concepts of "fictive" and vision is relevant to political forms of silencing and of producing social invisibility. The Czechoslovak Communist state aimed to make Mukls socially invisible, to deface them.

Analysis of torture from historical perspectives teaches us that torture has a long history and that its meanings and its raison d'être change over time (Asad 1997, Foucault 1977, Rejali 1994). Rejali posed two questions: "Do the accounts of political violence that we have developed over the past century have any real capacity to direct us in a world in which one out of every three governments tortures its citizens?" and "Do these accounts have any real explanatory or even moral significance in such a world, or are they just consolations in the face of events we cannot fully understand?" (Rejali 1994:2). My response to these questions, based on outcomes from my research about Czech political prisoners, is that detailed accounts of political violence are relevant. I agree with Talal Asad's skeptical view of generating a universal discourse about torture as inhumane and degrading treatment. I see an ethnography of pain and cruelty as a possibility for seeing and better understanding "how relevant practices are actually conducted in different traditions" (Asad 1997:304). I perceive cruelty as "a failure of specific virtues or as an expression of particular voices" (Asad 1997:304), rather than just simply the violation of rights.

The state's cruelty was materialized in the StB archive. Archival production impacts directly on political prisoners' subjectivities. For the StB, the process of constructing the archive while suppressing the actual physical archive of personal files was the significant political strategy underlying the state's violent ritual of silencing. Archival records from the interrogations were central to the relationship between political prisoners and the state. This was true during their time in prison as well as after their release. Archival production, whether an actual physical archive or an archive as a metaphorical location of knowledge, has a significant role in the post-socialist reconciliation. The process of making the StB archive visible and transparent was driven by a nationwide future hope. For me, reading the archives, as an alternative memory in a Guhaian and Aminian way,[1] and as texts within the texts, they proved a useful linguistic method for revealing the multi-leveled character of the archives in the context of Czechoslovakian and Czech political discourse.

FACING THE ARCHIVE

Arrest followed by interrogations was the beginning of the state's project of archive making. The interrogations became one of the regime's ways to establish its power rooted in the process of making an archive. The archive making, for the political prisoners, was closely tied to acts of torture. When physical torture was practiced, the archive was made, regardless of whether a tortured prisoner responded verbally, signed the paper admitting betrayal, or was silenced. The archive produced during the interrogations is embodied in the state's violent ritual of silencing. Interrogators strove to obtain prisoners' confessions to often-fictive crimes against the regime's ideology.

The original aim of interrogation, getting information from a suspect, is designed to have a long-lasting effect on him. The archival records from the interrogations are central to the relationship between the political prisoner and the state. For the state police the process of making the archive, the actual written personal file, was the significant locus for establishing its political power. The practitioners of torture who wrote in the prisoner's file, or report, were rewarded for accumulating successful records. It did not matter that the records of interrogation were fictive constructs. The falsification of motive, getting information from suspects, was central to the fictionalization of power. Confession, then, was an inversion of the absent past and the body's present. Archival production impacted directly on political prisoners' subjectivities.

Loebl, one of the arrested party members, wrote, "Every day we constructed some new crime. It was really very easy: we simply took something that I had really done, and said that I did it to destroy Socialism or the party" (Loebl 1976: 137). The personal files of the prisoners, as recorded by interrogators, became the secret StB archive. Based on the Mukls' testimony: *psali tam co chtěli* (they wrote what they pleased); the interrogators wrote anything they wished. "During each leisurely five to six hours of interrogation, every day except Sunday, Kohoutek wrote some six pages of confessions" (Loebl 1976:143). And Loebl continues: "After each confession, he compiled a short synopsis, which he called by the Russian name, *svodka*, in which he summed up what I had confessed on that day and how much progress he had made with me. These reports were sent to the teachers" (Loebl 1976:143). Each Mukl had a written file documenting the interrogations. The written record or report from interrogation became a narrative text, a survival narrative, constructed to provide truth for the interrogators, that truth which the prisoner had to learn to recite for the trial. It also became a document, a separate entity, stored at the state police archive.

Loebl wrote: "I was taken once again to the large office of the Russian interrogator. He said that his patience was at an end. Either I will confess tomorrow morning, or they would make me confess. He spoke to me slowly in his even, nasal voice: 'We want you to admit that you have been and are an agent of Tito, of world Jewry, and of the Anglo-American imperialists. And we want a confession and a description of how, with whom, and on whose orders you have done what you have done.' I told him I did not know what he was talking about" (Loebl 1976:80).

Loebl's confession not only reveals his participation in the process but also reveals how the fictive political power of the regime was embodied in the archive. For political prisoners, such as Loebl, the archive constitutes many contradictions. File making during the interrogations was surrounded by se-crecy and slowly constructed through endless hours of torture. This archive became a text in which interrogators constructed files with false admissions and forced prisoners to memorize their own accusations. "The treatment we received contained a combination of brutality and scientific calculation. It was a very sophisticated method. They played with pain and with time. They knew how to focus the attention of a physically weakened prisoner, and, by gradual deprivation, by cutting off all sense perceptions of the prisoner's mind" (Loebl 1976:140). In Mukls' memories such intentional strategies were described and remembered. For example, Milu, with whom I have had many informal conversations about interrogations, was aware of these strate-gies and in particular, the disruption of time. She told me, "In my memory the interrogations left a destroyed and confused sense of time. Part of the time Bohoušek, who arrested me, was with me, and often there were two or three others, and they were making noise. They screamed more and more, they hit the table with different things, they kicked my chair, until the chair tipped over with me in it, simply they were deafening me and threatening me. They took turns throughout the night and several times forced me to walk around the room until my legs were swollen and blue. Once during the walking, I collapsed and then felt a gentle touch, it was the doctor."

Reading Milu's narratives we can see the state's action upon prisoners' bodily senses. From Milu's torture narratives it is also evident how language, in relation to time and space, is used like an instrument to torture Milu's body. The relationship between language, death and silence is critical for the formation of a new discourse. As Feldman put it, "Language, death and silence are the three points of the interrogation triangle that govern the relations between the interrogator and his prisoner" (Feldman 1991:120). Milu, like many others, testified about the interrogators' voices switching from tough to soft mode, from asking questions about places and names, to humiliating and threatening verbal attacks. The language switch was practiced in two ways: either one actor switched from one voice to another, or two different interrogators divided their roles between good guy and bad guy. Fragmentation of speech was built into the interrogators' strategy, not only by employing multiple interrogators, but also by calling different witnesses into the interrogation room to testify. Milu remembers this:

> During one interrogation I put my head down from exhaustion, after awhile they shook me and screamed at me: "What color coat did you wear in Vinohrady, the gray one or blue one?" I was there, but unlike other women, I didn't make a mistake. I said, "What are you talking about?" During one interrogation they called in two witnesses and everything happened in such a strange way. The sculptor who was shivering when he saw me and said: "I can't take this on my conscience," and so they took him away. The second witness was the woman, who when she walked in the room calmly said, "No, it wasn't this lady." When I met her later in the showers she was apologetic, for dragging me into this. I asked her why she didn't say anything. She said, "I walked in the room and could see written on your back that you didn't say anything."

Milu in her narrative expressed how the possibility of a breakdown was one of the characteristic conditions of the interrogation's rhythm. I found a similar expression in Loebl's text: "The confession itself was a kind of breakdown; it was an expression of defeat, an acknowledgment of a situation that the prisoner did not have the strength to overcome" (Loebl 1976:140). Feldman conceptualized this relationship between physical torture and language when he wrote, "For the narrator, the cumulative sequence of beatings and attempted mutilations becomes a narrative of survival—a journey past language and the body and a return to language and the body that coincides with the recitation of the oral history" (Feldman 1991:119). Mukls' agency, expressed in narratives, is marked by violent acts during the interrogations. It is a symbolic pattern in all Mukls' memories, whether or not they resisted when reaching this point during the confession. Mukl František remembers reaching the point of a breakdown,

> During the interrogation, if they wanted testimony they were always in a group. They jumped at me all at once. Whoever could beat me and slap me, did, they were in a group. My nose was broken and I was bleeding. I was exhausted because they took me for interrogations day and night.
>
> When I returned to my cell I couldn't eat. My nose and teeth were broken. It was terror. They were convinced that they are fighting for the truth of Communism, and in that name they can do what they want.

Practically I was not organized, but before the war I was active in the *Lidová Strana* (Peoples Party—a Catholic political party) and didn't inform them about it during the interrogations. I was physically tortured. They forced me to admit what I had not done. I resisted, but then I couldn't anymore.

After the interrogations I was always alone in the cell. They put me in the cell previously occupied by Deputy Sachar, who was arrested for disagreement with the socialization of villages. He didn't make it through the interrogations and hanged himself in the cell. Because they put me in the same cell, they suggested that would be my fate as well.

František's testimony about physical and psychological torture, the torturers' use of the notions of space, time, and pressure to produce a survivors' language, a confession, provide insight into the discourse surrounding the formation of his subjectivity. In his memory, passing through the terror designed to generate a confession, to get the prisoner to speak, the interrogator targeted František's sense of touch, sound, time, and space. Other Mukls, just like František, spoke about their loss of a sense of vision, intensity of sound, degradation of touch, and disorder of time and space. František resisted for a while, but in the end the "techniques of petrification" (Feldman 2001:137) worked and his will was broken. The disorientation of František's sense of what was real served as an instrument of torture. His confession was transformed into narratives of survival, a new location for his agency. Some Mukls, like František, when remembering this moment of breakdown, lowered their voices, their narratives were surrounded by a painful peace they had developed over the years as a way to cope. I agree with Feldman, in Foucault's sense, that the state's production of subjects is also a self-production of the state. In this location where, "two metaphysical and intangibles" (Feldman 2001:115) are intersecting, the captive body is like a dual passageway for the state and its other(s).

Archival production reached beyond the time frame of interrogations in prison and continued until 1989, when the Communist regime in Czechoslovakia fell. After 1989, the state police (StB) archive was opened to the public. Czech and Slovak people focused their attention on the archive in the hope of finding a place of historical truth about our past. The files from the StB archive were published, discussed and used to determine who was an informant or agent for the regime.

The archive was used again in the post-Communist state to prove individual guilt or innocence of betrayal and to reveal his or her morality to the public eye. People were obsessed with the secrets in the StB records. Despite popular knowledge about the regime's mastery of fictive narratives, Czechs were anxious to learn what the regime thought of them. The archive, a process started by the StB, manifested in the forms of torture and interrogations, continues to be a political project. An archive as a commodity, a fetish possessing the power of secrets, often maintained by rumors, is also the location of fictive political power, and above all, has become a location for a continuous process of claiming moral and ethical truth. Only this time, the archive as a fetish is tossed from one political location to the other, while its fiction remains unchanged.

The archive, materialized in written form, remained the location of fictive political power in the 1990s, understood by the general public as a place of moral truth. The acknowledgment of the fictive character of Mukls' personal files within the state police archive has a crucial significance for understanding the recovery process after 1989. The StB archive is often viewed as the ultimate secret place of historical truth reflective of one's purity, morality and ethics during the dark past. Purity here is measured by Mukls' strength to face death and by their ability to resist; this is the case with every single interrogation in this historical context. Resistance is very ambiguous in the context of torture, but is always a matter of agency in negotiation with death. In this light, the use of the StB archive to define historical truth is misleading. In the post-totalitarian Czech Republic the concepts of desired truth often clash with the unavoidable fictive character of the archive. The strategic secrecy of the totalitarian state in the past complicates the reconciliation today. From the Mukls' perspective, continuity of the "evil," the state terror and its fiction, is present in archival knowledge whether in the form of memory or in a material archive. For these reasons, I view the investigation of the role of the archive to be critical for an understanding of political fiction lived by Mukls.

THE POWER OF THE SECRET, BODY, AND VISION

Invisible to the public while interrogated, transported back and forth between prisons and police stations, Mukls found themselves in a vacuum. Social invisibility to other citizens and being surrounded by secrecy were instrumental for developing alienation between Mukls and the rest of society. Secrecy was interwoven into the very nature of violent rituals, from arrest to camp confinement, practiced by the state. The place and condition of the arrested member of the family remained a secret. During the interrogation stage, when prisoners were transported from Pankrác prison[2] to interrogation rooms in the Bartolomějská police station, secrecy was built into the politics or practice of torture. The secrecy of torture is, according to Foucault, key to understanding the change in the form of punishment from public ritual and performative character to modern secret. "Punishment, then, will tend to become the most hidden part of the penal process" (Foucault 1977:9). According to Foucault, under modern forms of punishment, the punished is to be defaced and cannot be faced by others. Secrecy, a modern condition of punishment, penetrated Mukls' everydayness; secrecy became an inseparable part of Muklhood. A number of Mukls spoke about their regular and invisible journey from Pankrác to Bartolomějská:

> **Albína:** They beat us quite a lot. They told me to take my earrings out and then they repetitively slapped me in the face. It was scary. When they were transporting us from Pankrác to Bartolomějská, the bus was full of women. It was strange, they were transporting us through Prague and people were coming in and out of shops, carrying packages, and laughing. The public didn't notice. I was thinking how can I understand that they—people—didn't know, that they couldn't care less about us and how we suffer. We were disturbed to see how the whole nation ignored us; we expected the nation to stand by us. I was in the arrest cell a long time. I was waiting for the interrogations. They were bad. It was only later that the public learned what was happening.

Albína described the state's active policing as it "circulates in secret" (Asad 1997:289). The secrecy became a technique for generating political power, which subjected prisoners to rites of passage. Albína clearly remembered their (the prisoners') sudden defacement, their loss of social visibility to others. Analysis of her transport and interrogation narratives reveals the role of visual discourse in the mechanics of torture. Vision, linked here to the mechanics of power, has become an instrument of what Feldman called "scopic regime" (Feldman 2001:52).

Albína's testimony marks the form of pain inflicted by the scopic regime in the process of making a Mukl. While this condition of defacement as social invisibility in public and private spheres continues throughout Mukls' interrogations, trials and later in the camps, other new forms of defacement also emerged during the violent ritual. Mukls' faces were covered so that the interrogator remained anonymous to the prisoner. The invisibility of the interrogator depersonalized the violent acts of torture. The unrecognizable faces enhanced the Mukls' pain. Feldman discussed similar dynamics in the context of Irish prisoners. As he pointed out, prisoners' loss of vision also impacted on their sense of time. Feldman proposed the idea that the removal of time does not just cause disorientation and loss of points of reference, but "the simulation of death" (Feldman 2001:137). This closeness to death, as he later discussed, has a transitional purpose. A prisoner facing death is experiencing a "political rite of passage" (Feldman 2001:142). The most powerful instrument for the simulation of death was the manipulation of the scopic regime. Vision that has been politicized falls also into the genealogy of the real and the fictive.

Vision, visibility, invisibility as domains of political discourse and the reflection of the fictive, mimetic and its conversion to a means of distribution of political power are subjects discussed by Michael Taussig (Taussig 1999). Taussig's "space of death" is a metaphor modeled on Dante's journey into darkness. By "space of death" Taussig means a space of transformation through which closeness to death can become a "vivid sense of life." The production of fear is, for Taussig, also the production of self-consciousness and loss of the self through conformity to authority (Taussig 1987:7). Like Feldman, Taussig (in the South American context) sees acts of interrogation as crucial to the cultural elaboration of fear and terror.

From Feldman's perspective, the power of invisibility, created through defacement, as a cultivation of non-seeing, is part of the dominant power of violence. Mukls' social invisibility—defacement, openly discussed by Albína and by others, becomes a "depictive vehicle" (Feldman 2001:59) for the expression of violence. Defacement continued into the events of the trial and life in the camps afterwards. This politicized vision was defined by Feldman: "In terms of the creation of fear and dominance there is very little difference here between physical assault and scopic power; each reinforces and simulates the other" (Feldman 2001:59).

In the context of Muklhood, the concept of defacement is not limited to social invisibility, not being seen, but defacement also applies to prisoners' denied or lost vision. A lost sense of vision during the interrogations became an instrumental form of bodily torture but was not the only torment inflicted on the prisoners. Torture took many forms: loud sounds, interrogators' voices, pounding on the table, beating and burning of naked bodies, depriving prisoners food and water, and sensory deprivation; all of these forms of torture were experienced by both males and females. The lost sense of sight intensified the senses of touch and hearing. Darkness, the manipulation of vision, intensified punishment. When taken to the interrogation room, and during the process, prisoners' eyes were often covered. The faces of interrogators and the prison space were invisible for the Mukl. In darkness the sense of time as well as the sense of vision were lost. Hilda and Čeněk remember:

Hilda: Interrogations were horrible. They forced us to get naked. In the cells when we heard the sound of keys we had to put a black cloth over the eyes, so that we couldn't see any one of the interrogators.

Čeněk: The interrogators are anonymous to me because I was interrogated with eyes covered, and I was naked.

In Hilda and Čeněk's memory, the passage to Muklhood is marked by lost vision, nakedness and secrecy. Another defacement results when a Mukl cannot see, but is seen. Created through the defacement of the human eye, the scopic power becomes an inevitable part of the structures of dominant power and violence. I agree with Feldman: "In terms of creation of fear and dominance there is very little differentiation here between physical assault and scopic power; each reinforces and simulates the other" (Feldman 2001:59). Just as, in Albína's testimony, the invisibility of prisoners to the public was part of the strategic secrecy of the state, so too was the invisibility of the interrogators to the naked prisoners. The nakedness and loss of the sense of vision of the interrogated emerged as a voiced pattern not only in Hilda and Čeněk's torture narratives, but also in many others. Loss of vision during the interrogation became a strategy for increasing Mukls' physical pain. (I will also discuss this in a later section as a form of the memory of humiliation.) The anonymity of interrogators depersonalized the relationship between Mukl and torturer.

One of the Mukls I spoke to once said to me regarding the relationship between the guards and Mukls, "To us the guards were just guards, not people, and for them we were just bugs." To Mukls this dehumanizing relationship was established the moment they entered prison. Incoming prisoners were subjected to a routine search, which included orders to strip naked. Later in the camps, when Mukls were subjected to torture, they were often stripped naked and then beaten. Some, based on testimonies from Jáchymov,[3] were, after the severe beating of their naked bodies, splashed with water that froze on them when the weather there was cold. During the interrogations a Mukl's body, just like his face, became part of the state political project.

"The surface of the body is the stage where the state is made to appear as an effective material force" (Feldman 1991:115).

REMEMBERING HUMILIATION

Mukls' subjectivity, shaped by humiliation and pain, is especially transparent from their torture narratives. Mukls' testimonies are forms of memory. Remembered humiliation is one of the Mukls' significant recollections of interrogations. Lawrence Langer in *The Ruins of Memory* (Langer 1991) distinguished between different kinds of remembering the Holocaust. Langer argues that while the listener may take testimony as a smooth and flowing chronicle of personal history, narrators recalled the memory of trauma as what he called disruptive memory, the memory controlled by "contemporality" (Langer 1991:3). He saw a rupture between survivors' memory of Nazi camps and life afterwards. Talal Asad suggested that the perception of torture or cruel, inhuman and degrading practices, the very concept of pain and suffering, and its moral and legal judgment, derive from historically and culturally shaped ideas. In his view transcultural judgments are to be clarified and inclusive of careful examination of how concepts of cruelty are constructed. In this section I will present evidence about specific instances of cruelty, remembered by Mukls and linked to particular cultural values.

While being interviewed, Mukls told their stories chronologically, but in between interviews, during our informal conversations or at meetings with other Mukls, their memories were more random. Small episodes after arrest, or from time served in the prisons, often became a point of reference when expressing their everyday experiences in the present as a story told "out of time" (Langer 1991).

BODY AND THE STATE

Jiří K's testimony stood out from all the others. In the prisons, his was the position of a medical doctor. Dr. K went through a number of different locations. In the early part of his imprisonment, in what Mukls call the stone prisons, he was treated brutally. He was imprisoned with *retribucni*, Nazis imprisoned after liberation in 1945, and then transferred to Leopoldov prison.[4] As a doctor he witnessed suffering in its extreme. Dr. K himself experienced injuries from being severely beaten. He also, from his position as a medical doctor, frequently (compared to other Mukls) witnessed the consequences of the physical abuse of others. His testimony concerns a period when he was treating injured and ill Mukls.[5] When he spoke to me about being forced to participate in torture, he remembered his humiliation and witnessing the humiliation of other prisoners in a more direct way than the other Mukls. He began his testimony by describing the conditions in the prison:

I think it is important that I will mention what I experienced in the prisons. These prisons were tremendously cruel, inhuman, humanity disappeared, they treated a man like in the Nazi concentration camps. I lived through the biggest horrors in Bory (a prison in the city of Plzeň), in the so-called *Štráf Komando C*), where they sent people about whom they were unsure if they could come back to society. These people were treated horribly. Such a person had to live in some small cell, where he slept on rags, never came out, was beaten and tortured by means of starvation. He had to strip eighty kilos of dirty feathers and in such health-damaging environment he had to sit, live and sleep. Sometimes he became the target of the guards.

After that he switched and spoke about his own experience.

For example, what happened to me was that I was poisoned and had an intestinal infection, which caused me frequent, bloody diarrhea. There was no lavatory, one had to use the back corner of the room. I tried to get to the doctor. I was feeling already very sick and as a result of the anemia I could hardly stay on my feet. I gave the ticket to the guard for the doctor, and the guard kicks me in my stomach and said, "You are just a lazy shit." The next day I tried again, and the third day they came and took me to the hospital. It was not easy. I had to wait in line in the hallway. My head was spinning, so I leaned against the wall. That became the source of negative attention of a guard, whose name was Tichý, and he was from a small village outside of Klatovy (a city in the southwest region of the Czech Republic). He jumped on me, threw me on the floor, at the time I weighed only fifty kilos, and he said, "You'd like to escape, you piece of shit," and then he called me a dirty intellectual and said that he will take care of me. He begins to step on me with his boots that were framed with metal. He was stepping all over my head and genitals on purpose. I will shorten this and tell you what he did to me: he broke two vertebrae, damaged my right eye which is blind as a result of this, broke my elbow and injured my penis. I was lying on the floor in a way that they thought I was dead. They put me on the gurney and were pushing me to the room where they store dead bodies. To my luck I lifted my head and one of the guards saw it and said, "He is alive." After that they took me to the cell where they threw me on the floor.

It seems impossible, but I did survive it. After that I had to strip eighty kilo of feathers again, and when I didn't meet the norms I was put in a so-called *korekce*, correction. Those men were getting only half of a portion of food, and at night drunken guards tortured us the way I described it above.

Dr. K's position changed when he was sent to a transitional prison, Leopoldov, where he was to serve as a doctor. This historic prison was used by the regime for Mukls before they were sent to work camps, or if they were considered highly dangerous and confined to solitude. It was in Leopoldov that he witnessed different forms of humiliation and pain when he was forced to practice medicine with a lack of medical supplies and equipment. He recalls,

Later on I was transported to Leopoldov. That was a prison with a very specific function: a death camp. Guards were saying to us there: "From here you will leave only with your feet ahead of you or in the wooden box." Later on I found what was really on their minds. I was called to the commander's office. They had a meeting, and I was waiting in the next room when I overheard the discussion they had over the methods of how to kill prisoners, because the number of the prisoners was increasing. The suggested methods were brutal, and in the end someone said, "Let's do it like the Germans did, injections to the heart." When I heard this I was terrified. Then they called me in and asked me, "Doctor, do you know how to give an injection to the heart?" Before I could finish my reply the commandant said, "You know, so you can go now!"

One day the guards took me. I thought I am going to be tortured, but instead I was taken to the hospital. It was a former horse barn with nothing in it except some old cupboards. I was sitting there for a while, and then they called me to go to the officer. The officer said, "Some idiot swallowed a spoon, go and operate since you are a doctor!"

I thought that the space I saw was just the space before the operation room, but there was nothing else there. I asked again if this is the place that I will operate, and two medical people present in the room nodded their heads. I sat down and wrote the list of things I will need from a nearby hospital. After that they called me again, and the commander then was angry and said, "I told you to operate and if not you will go to 'special training,'" which was unbearable solitary confinement, where you have to sleep on the concrete floor and get to eat only three spoons of pasta for the day. I knew it was bad. I went to that barn and placed two pieces of the wooden boxes and put plywood over it. When they brought the poor fellow in I said, "Dear friend, the operation that I will do is nothing extra difficult, but you have to be patient because of the conditions here, and mainly I can't give you complete anesthesia." I opened his stomach and took out the spoon, and he survived. Since then I stayed in this so-called hospital."

One person had a stomach tumor from repetitive kicking by the guards; the tumor grew inside his stomach and this caused bleeding. It took several days before I accomplished getting him into the hospital. I went there by myself with the assistant and begged the guard to hurry. That was a mistake. In the solitary cells was a guard named Juriš, a tremendously brutal person. He did terrible things to this poor fellow; he kicked him repetitively to his stomach with heavy boots reinforced with metal. From the poor man sprayed a stream of blood and then he lost consciousness. I put him on a gurney. I had a horrible transfusion system. I was gathering blood in such a small container, added *citrak*, and then mixed it together carefully. I knew approximately what kind of blood types the patients had, and so I gave them the shots to the vein. This particular person I gave a large amount of the blood and operated on him the next day.

Not everybody was lucky to get to the hospital. I witnessed hundreds of people dying during torture. When someone needed an operation I had to detect the commander's good mood; otherwise he would say, "Let him perish." But not always could I help.

There was once one former pilot from the war, who suffered from a lung infection. He was in a solitary cell. I managed to get him to the hospital. When I took his temperature the thermometer showed 40°C. I went to the commandant and showed him the thermometer. He takes a look and then says, "I will test him." Then this happened: the commandant forces this poor man to walk outside in a circle. It was in February, and outside it was freezing, the man had a 40°C fever, was dressed lightly, and had only sneakers on. "Quickly, quickly," cried the commander, and I was horrified. I was on my knees begging him to send this man to the hospital. After awhile the poor fellow collapsed on the ground and died. They didn't allow me to even come to him. They just scraped him under the ground, typical of their manner.

In Doctor K's testimony, the memory of his own suffering is overshadowed by the memory of the pain of others. Suffering of other inmates was at the center of Dr. K's everyday life in the prison. Based on his narratives it is evident that he was often in a position between Mukl and the prison guards, the establishment. During one of our talks, Dr. K revealed that there was a time when he was called to fix a prisoner in between interrogations, so that he would be ready for the next torturing.

When Dr. K spoke, compared to other testimonies, he spoke fast. The tone of his firm voice made an impression on me, as if he had spoken about this many times before our interview. Yet he spoke about particular cruelty with a focus on detail and with compassion when reporting on the pain of others.

Since then, I kept the interview with Dr. K in my memory, and with time I began to wonder about the ambiguity of his position. It was not so much his particular experiences that I went over in my mind, but the inter-textual silences in his narratives. His silence about his painful medical mission was embodied in the register of his voice.

Scarry suggested that it is the nature of torture, that medicine and law, health and justice, are side by side, and that they are an "institutional elaboration of body and state" (Scarry 1985:42). Further, she defined this experience as a deconstruction of the institution of medicine and law (Scarry 1985:42), and she argues that just like law, medicine is "unmade by being made once an actual agent of pain" (Scarry 1985). Dr. K's position, such a paradoxical twist, between being the agent of healing and the "agent of pain" (Scarry 1985), traumatized him. He was forced to practice medicine where his patients' association with pain was not with the promise of healing, but with the infliction of pain by the state on patients' bodies. Feldman elaborates on Scarry and writes: "the creation of state hegemony in the process of torture as based on the detachment and transfer of political meaning and significative capacities from the body of the tortured to the instruments of torture which become fetishized symbols of the state" (Feldman 1991:143). Lawrence Langer points out that remembering is difficult, but speaking is even more so, because it violates the condition of speechlessness in which the witness experienced the specific event. He argued that "telling this story is more than a form of testimony, designed to inform others: it is also a self-examination, a full-time effort to exonerate oneself of guilt concerning a deed for which one bears no responsibility in the context of event" (Langer 1991:87).

In telling his story, Dr. K had to return, over and over, to the conditions he had experienced as a doctor in the camps. I read, in his cohesive and well-articulated narratives, beyond speech, a deep silence. It is the silence of witnessing, as well as participation. Dr. K's memory of the humiliation of self is also the memory of witnessing and being forced to participate in the humiliation of others. The position from which he speaks is not an easy one. Susanna Trnka pointed out that it is not always language alone through which pain is expressed, but in many accounts pain is "felt by others" (Trnka 2008:20). Further she suggests that "articulations of pain may result in its collective embodiment" (Trnka 2008:20). In her ethnographic account in Fiji, Trnka shows the potential of language to do more than convey the events of violence, and how it can simultaneously "stimulate collective embodiments of pain" (Trnka 2008:20).

The relationship between words, silences and meaning sheds light on the complexities of experiences like those of Dr. K. He was unique not only in his role in the camps, but also in the process of rehabilitation. In the late 1960s, Dr. K was called to testify about cruelty and inhumane treatment in the prisons and camps during the 1950s. The decade of the 1960s was a brief period in Czechoslovakia when the regime was weakened by economic crises, the deaths of some of the radical Communist leaders, and the new generation of leading members of the Communist Party who proclaimed the politics of socialism with a human face. The 1960s political transformation in Czechoslovakia is associated with the term *Czech Spring* or *Prague Spring*.[6] The resulting freedom was relative, but nonetheless, there was an attempt at re-evaluation of the 1950s political terror. Mukls demanding rehabilitation broke the silence about the political violence in the 1950s. Many were able to enter the application process and participate in the investigations of individual cases, but only a few received a full rehabilitation. Dr. K was very active in this process: "In the year sixty-eight I served as a witness in many different places: in the courthouse, the Ministry of Health, but then came the Soviet Invasion." The rehabilitation process was interrupted by a new Soviet occupation of Czechoslovakia in August 1968. Mukls, once again, were silenced by the state. "After the 1989 Revolution nobody was interested in what happened in Leopoldov."

When I met him, at the end of his life, Dr. K was actively involved in health initiatives for the aging Mukls. His life was invested in advocacy for medical justice for other Mukls. I will return to the subject of aging and Muklhood in the last chapter.

GENDERED PAIN OF OTHERS

Gendered pain holds a significant place in the Mukls' interrogation narratives. While remembering the humiliation, other Mukls spoke about the pain of others. Neither men nor women were interested in a heroic representation of themselves, but they frequently referred to pain as attached in particular ways to the male or female body. Men often said women suffered more because of their female bodies and the menstrual cycle requiring hygiene; women often said men suffered more because they were beaten more and humiliation was hard on their male pride. Women also spoke about female "instincts" that allowed them to survive the cruelty of the interrogators. Albína told me, "Men were beaten more. I saw how they were carried like baggage, covered with blood; they were not capable of walking. I think for the men it was worse. I took it with passivity when they were slapping and kicking me, but the men had tendencies to resist. Psychologically we (women) were able to take it better. We try to accept and survive with a woman's instinct."

In Albína's narratives, her own pain is not an isolated memory, it is as though it is stored in the communal archive of pain. This archival space for pain has significance for Mukls' subjectivity. For Mukls, the violation of a physical, psychological and cultural way of being is affected by pain inflicted on them by the state. The Mukls' concept of gender is based on cultural notions of "male" and "female" roles as defined by Czech society prior to their arrest. Albína, under the condition of cultural construction of gender, reasons her own resistance to pain as the result of female instinct, which she perceived as the measure of tolerance for pain during the rites of passage which she translates to "men" and "women" labor division for pain. Fiona Ross found similar conditions in the context of South African reconciliation processes. She witnessed women's representations of their own physical experience of violence and perceived their struggle as a particular type of knowledge (Ross 2003). Ross reasoned that women's remembering the pain of others and their silence about their own pain is based on culturally constructed ideas about bodily pain and gender roles.

Czech Muklyněs spoke carefully, in detailed ways, about the interrogation performances. They often emphasized the role of psychological, as well as physical, torture directed towards de-feminizing as well as dehumanizing them. I noticed in women's torture narratives multiple registers in their voices. In addition to a voice describing a diachronic flow of torture acts, they also speak about the internal voice, hidden in the silence they maintained during interrogations. Silence during the interrogations is presented in their narratives as a figure of speech, and a double register, the silent and hidden internal voice. It was through this strong, internal voice by which they seem to keep a sense of agency that empowered them. In her memoir, Muklyně Dagmar Šimková repetitively returns to the concept of gendered pain. She opened one of the chapters in her book, "Most of us survived with a healthy mind, and it was determined by the fact that we are women. Not that women had easy conditions in prison, there was no difference in the level of cruelty, but women developed different survival instincts compared to men. Every woman has the ability to build her own space, nest, always ready to fight with small and big problems (Šimková 1994).

Šimková emphasized the gender differences, but she also wrote about gendered pain in relation to different forms of humiliation used to degrade her during interrogations. "Interrogators favorite games were directed to make us hate ourselves. A woman had to be shamed for her femininity, she has to be deprived of her gender" (Šimková 1991).

Šimková, and other Muklyněs, testify about the intentional de-feminizing of their bodies: making them wear oversized, male prisoners' clothing, not allowing them to use the toilet, making them feel as if they were *bezpohlavní*, de-sexed. She wrote about one long-lasting interrogation in which her human failure to control her bladder was characterized as a female failure: "I was turning red, the tears were running down my cheeks, I asked them over and over if I could go to the bathroom. After another hour my body gave up, I soiled the carpet. The agent screamed: 'throw her out—that wet bitch'" (Šimková 1994).

In response to gendered forms of humiliation, psychological pain inflicted on her and others through strategic desexualization, Šimková described various ways women resisted the interrogators' efforts: "For agents we are bitches, smelly discharge, whores, beasts. Our anti-poison was mutual kindness and attachment. We called ourselves by diminutives. We are "Marušky," "Pepičky," "Aničky," regardless of age and body shapes. We are ladies. We are watching our moves, expressions, intonations, self-control, that gives us the strength to keep a sense of respect. We call this *šustění hedvabím*, crinkling or rustling silk."

Some Muklyněs across the boundaries of different prison locations spoke about mutual care, gentle language and grace in manners. Others spoke about their daily rituals of washing their bodies, clothes and cells or weekly beautification sessions, *šustění hedvabím*. These rituals of cleansing and purifying were for them a serious labor of self-gradation and preservation of their dignity. Dignifying rituals had a cohesive and bonding effect on Muklyněs' mutual relatedness, and it gave them a new sense of bonds and belonging.

In her book *Shattering Silence*, Begona Aretxaga discusses how Irish women prisoners used their bodies during the "dirty protest." They reversed cultural notions of the clean feminine body in a radical protest against the British attempts to criminalize them. She wrote, "For more than one year thirty-two women lived in tiny cells without washing themselves, amid their own menstrual blood and bodily waste" (Aretxaga 1997:122). Further she discussed how this sort of protest triggered by the symbolism of menstrual blood shifted the construction of gender and sexual differences in the Irish context, as women protesters worked their way through their femininity into the public discourse (see Aretxaga 1997).

Veena Das wrote about the location of women's bodies as a part of the political project during communal violence in India at the time of partition. She wrote, "The bodies of the women were surfaces on which texts were to be written and read—icons of the new nations" (Das 1997:85). Czechoslovak women prisoners, just like Irish women, identified distinct ways they were, in contrast to men, tortured and humiliated. They were routinely subjected to humiliation, not only as political prisoners, but also as women. Yet I agree with Aretxaga that "it is soul not body that is the target of disciplinary power" (Aretxaga 1997: 130) and that it is subjectivity, which is transformed through the bodily discipline of the prisons. Subjectivity, then, is not reduced to relations between power and rationality, "rational techniques of control" (Aretxaga 1997), but remains a dynamic charged with elements of women prisoners' active agency.

In the Mukls case, the bodies of women and men became part of the political project, but it was women's bodies, especially, that became the surface for texts written and read as symbols of greater humiliation. The state used women's bodies in different ways than they used men's bodies. Different forms of humiliation took place through culturally designed notions of femininity and masculinity, and resulted in the desexualization of women. But both men and woman spoke of the pain and humiliation endured by the opposite sex. Mukls' shared, humiliating memories of the gendered pain of others often reveals their resistance to constructions of themselves on the basis of degradation, but it also reflected the cultural frames for masculine and feminine roles. One of the Mukls, Jaroslav, spoke about the episode from Pankrác prison: "When we took a shower we had to get undressed in the cells and then in a group walk through the prison hallway. One time I remember our male group was passing a female group coming from the shower. We saw the group of naked women prisoners coming towards us in the hallway. Both groups exchanged enthusiastic hollering and jumping up and down. There was not a sense of the erotic, but solidarity. I felt so helpless that I couldn't, as a male, keep the women from such humiliation, that I couldn't protect women."

The "degradation ceremony" (Goffman 1961) failed. Mukls and Muklyněs resisted constructions of themselves. As some indicated, Mukls' sense of humiliation and punishment through their bodies is influenced by their culturally and gender-constructed views. Mukls, in their narratives, measure the severity of pain and the tolerance for pain through culturally based gendered divisions of pain. I noticed that when remembering the humiliation of others, humiliated memory encompasses gendered pain. In our conversation Čeněk remembered the time before the trial: "I have to say it was the pain of the others that was the worst for me. Imagining pain inflicted on helpless others, especially women, was the worst for me. I was taken to Pankrác hospital at some point before my trial. There, I saw the women's hospital. They arrested pregnant women destined to deliver at the prison. From my window, I could see the wagons taking newborns for nursing across the courtyard. My friend, who was in a different part of the same prison, saw women sitting down under the gallows and nursing, because that was the only place with sunshine. These were hard things for me to take."

Čeněk's memory of humiliation, in spite of the severity of his own pain, claimed the pain of others. Čeněk was brutally tortured by the StB during his interrogations before his trial. They used different forms of torture to force him to collaborate. He was tied naked to a chair, beaten, and electrocuted. Interrogators tied his head with a wet cloth, burned his nostrils and ultimately swung his body from a balcony. All this was done to make him sign a confession, but he told me he did not. Now, in retrospect, he remembered the pain of others. He claimed that it was not his pain, but the pain of others that dominated his mind when he was in solitude and in between interrogations.

Mukls revealed in their testimonies that the condition of pain is not limited to one's body, but can be shared by others. In this sense the inflicted pain, as articulated in their testimonies, expands beyond the boundaries of one's body and in psychological ways is located in relatedness. Veena Das, in her dialog with Stanley Cavel on the subject of pain, explores the very same ideas, drawing from Wittgenstein, for her pain, is not limited to one's body, but can be located in relatedness.

THE POWER OF KINSHIP RELATEDNESS

People's ability to relate to others has been considered by many social scientists as a powerful measure of humanness. Many anthropologists, concerned with the impact of political violence on individuals and communities, have investigated the resulting transformation of social relations (Das and Kleinman 2001). They agree that in the midst of the worst horrors, people continue to live, to survive, and to cope. Contemporary ethnographies of violence often ask: What is the sense of everydayness or ordinary as lived under such circumstances, and how may people relate to others and become part of their own understanding of violence? When responding to this question the idea of "relatedness" and violence (Das 1997) proves to be a critical one to consider.

Based on many narratives, the continued fragmentation of kinship bonds by the state was a strategy of the totalitarian regime in Czechoslovakia. Families of the arrested were parted without exception. Some described one view in particular, the view from the Pankrác prison building into the courtyard

where, below the gallows, mothers nursed their newborn babies. Several
Mukls independently remember just like Hilda:

The courtyard outing was a generous gift from the prison institution to the new
mothers. It was a gift to the prisoners of fresh air. Fathers were not allowed.
These mothers were even arrested while pregnant, and a small number of
women who became pregnant after being raped by the guards. Each gave birth
in the prison and kept the child until the trial. Then the child was sent to her
family or to a socialist orphanage. The family could claim the child, but if their
family was considered unreliable, children were given up for adoption. Some
mothers lost contact and never found their children.

During the interrogations kinship bonds, family relatedness, became one of
the most powerful instruments for the exercise of state power over the political other. Čeněk spoke about this in his interrogation narratives: "Parallel to
my night interrogations they did a search of my home. After interrogations,
in the morning, they threw my things on the table in front of me, and I could
tell they had been at my house and had done a thorough search."

In addition to other forms of torture discussed in a previous section, here
Čeněk speaks about the connection to his family during torture. Čeněk's family relatedness, used by the state to extract information and a confession from
Čeněk, was a form of torture materialized through his personal things from
home. Found objects among Čeněk's personal possessions from his home
were used by the state in the interrogation room to signify to Čeněk its total
power over his familial space and relatedness.

The denial of contact with, or the intentional harming of, relatives was
one of the state's well-developed and often applied strategies to attempt
to achieve control over the relationship between Mukls and their relatives.
Albína remembers, "My husband died while I was in prison. They tortured
me with the denial of mail for three months, and then they threw the death
certificates on the table in front of me." Mukls' kinship relatedness, as many
indicated, made them vulnerable to totalitarian power. For example, manipulation of information about family was a strategy built into the interrogation
rituals. We can see this in Albína's testimony and in Čeněk's. The interrogators' acts signify to prisoners that the state controls their relatives' lives
outside of prison. The denial of contact with one's children became a form
of torture. Milu, in her written memoir of her time in Pankrác prison before
her trial, wrote, "My biggest fear was for Martin. When I left, he was around
twelve years old, when boys are inventing all kinds of things, on bikes, and I
can see him in my mind, how he is weaving somewhere between cars" (Holubová 1998:72). Anežka recalls that

Our children were left behind on their own after my husband and I were both arrested. They were seventeen. Our son was in the ceramics school and our daughter in the conservatory studying voice. They sent them to the factory. So they were alone. One friend took care of them because they moved them out of our home to the brewery cellar in Branik, but they, the children left and got a small flat. When I was interrogated in Pankrác I didn't know about my children for four months. They paid for this all their lives. They tried to threaten me, they said: If you don't cooperate we will make your son a pimp and your daughter a whore.

The uncertain future of her children, not knowing where they were and what was happening to them, was painful to Anežka. The interrogators used her motherhood as a means of torture. Anežka's family was fragmented. The everyday mothering of her own children was denied; interrogators tortured her through her motherhood. In her narratives of interrogation she mentioned another episode. "During the interrogations they wrote what they needed, not what I told them. I had a Russian interrogator, who had a revolver on the table. He was screaming at me: 'You bitch, I would like to shoot you,' he said that in the Czech language. Then he beat me so long until I told him 'I hope that your mother will one time experience what I had to, I could be your mother.' He stopped and didn't beat me any more." Anežka's words illustrate how, at the moment of violent interrogation, motherhood became an identity through which she could speak to the interrogator. When she was beaten her strong sense of self as a mother at the moment entered into the relationship between her and the guard. Her speech ruptured the aggression of the beater.

In the prison Anežka was one of the older prisoners. She is now remembered by younger Zdeňka: "I was one of the youngest; we were supporting each other. Anežka and Hilda, who were older and had children outside, both often combed my hair and patted me on my head. I couldn't understand it, only after many years I remembered. They needed it to express, somehow, love, they had to give love. It was the feeling that women have to give to someone and so new relations come about."

In testimonies like this one, parenthood is described by Mukls as lost to the regime, but also remembered as a type of relatedness that transformed Mukls' kinship bonds from outside to inside the prison. Based on Zdeňka's and other Muklynĕs' narratives from informal talks, older women prisoners, especially those who already had children outside of prison, often mothered women prisoners who were arrested in their youth. From Zdeňka's narratives we can see an early moment of a newly developing bond through the older women's mothering of younger female prisoners. Denial of kin relatedness, loss of children during imprisonment, not knowing about them during interrogations, all caused pain and fear. At the same time mothers, like Hilda and Anežka, expressed their pain and concern for their own children in their care for younger women prisoners. The loss was transformed and new forms of relations developed among the co-prisoners. The nature of relationships was transformed. The transformation, as I have shown, happened even during solitary confinement, indicating that solitude was never just solitude. The Mukls' sense of his or her interiority became the space into which the memory of the familial and ordinary from the past could enter.

Mukls and their children made two different references to the term *family*. They distinguish between family in terms of belonging to a nuclear family, understood in a Czech context as a social unit typically composed of husband, wife, and children, and belonging to a Mukls' family, constructed from commonality of experience. Family ties of the first type were systematically undermined by state violent acts. During violent rituals relatedness was used by the state as a means of punishment and torture. Ironically, at the very moment of such events, the memory of close relatives became for the Mukl a foundation for future hope. The regime tried to prevent individual Mukls from maintaining ties with their kin. Some Mukls lost connections with their kin, and others did not. But among those who did not, many developed new forms of family relatedness and belonging. This new family is valued on the same level as kinship ties. Their references to Mukls' family indicate that their shared experience bound them closely. To have been a Mukl becomes for many a claim to membership in a brotherhood and a sisterhood (I will return to this theme in Part II).

Mukls' memory of torture and kinship is not limited to the remembering of relatedness as a source of pain. They also remember how, in difficult moments, the sense of relatedness helps them. Milu remembered one of the examples of such connectedness: "When I came to the cell (after interrogation) I immediately fell asleep. In the dream I could hear my mother's voice: 'Miluško, you know what? Let's go to the garden that would be best of all.' Her voice was with me like that until they came for me again."

Milu claimed that, like herself, many prisoners who kept close relatives in mind during interrogations and torture were, as she put it, "in a better disposition." According to Milu, Mukls' consciousness of kin relatedness was empowering. The consciousness of relatedness to others was one of the aspects, but not the only one, that made the passage through the violent ritual possible.

Milu's case is also a good example of double remembering. Milu's voice as a mother indicated her fears for the son she left behind. Yet Milu's voice as a daughter drew comfort from the connection to her mother. Remembering her mother in moments of exhaustion from the interrogations was pleasant and comforting for her. At the time of her arrest she was a single mother working on her PhD. Her father was ill, and her mother had just emigrated with her older brother to France. When she was interrogated in prison, her son was in the state dormitory for adolescents. During our conversations Milu referred often to jail as a defining point in her life. Jail represented the division between her old and new subjectivity.

"When they interrogated me, I said that I don't know anything, I haven't done anything, and I don't know what they are talking about. I would say this, whether they interrogated me collectively or individually.

They forced me to walk around the cell until I collapsed. It was immediately after forty-eight when it was worst. Of course, I was scared, but I thought to myself as long as they are not beating me, it is fine. Also I had in my head all the stories from the world how people were tortured, so when a man was screaming at me, I thought it was nothing. I was not even thinking about collapsing. It was my own stubbornness."

Milu's son, Martin, expressed to me over the phone: "While in the prison, she denied everything. Even after many hours of interrogation she wouldn't make a mistake. She was driven by a sense of knowing that I needed her, so when she was interrogated she did everything that she could to get back to me. I lived as a child of Milu, who didn't confess—or conform to them. For my mother the experience of prison became the measure of relations. She used to tell me: I hope you will find a partner in life with whom you will know what that partner would do if you were in prison. Prison was a measure of a relationship for her. My mother, when she returned, was very angry with me for my bad grades, for stopping piano and English language lessons. She gave me hell, but underlying this was the unity of love."

In Milu's case, her resistance restores time and "a new body at the time of interrogation as a signal of the transformation of the interrogation experience into a political rite of passage" (Feldman 2001:142). Milu spoke about a strong sense of agency internalized during interrogations. This internal space was the domain of her remembering her relationship as mother to son, and also her relationship to her mother. For Milu, the experience of interrogations in prison, passing through a dark space, became a measure of relationships. Just like Milu, other Mukls spoke about internal agency, silence and pain while subjected to torture.

CONCLUSION

The strategic solitude at the moment of interrogation was, I argue, transformed and became a means of Mukls' survival, even perhaps of future hope for some of them. Interrogation narratives show Mukls' ability to maintain a sense of relating to others; connectedness was important to them. Remembering relatives became a mechanism of pain during torture, but also a possibility of resistance and future hope under state terror. Solitude, strategically maintained by the interrogators throughout the violent ritual passage and preparation of the Mukls' for trial, turned out to be instances of reverse power. Mukls' solitude, for some, was enriched by memory or dreams of relatedness and became significant for the possibility of future hope. Jiří Mucha wrote about the pleasant feeling resulting from remembering. "The memory of some little joy unexpectedly pierces your heart, and it suddenly stands for the whole complex concept of freedom" (Mucha 1967:21). Understanding the memory of pleasant things next to the memory of torture has been discussed by subaltern scholars as a potential multiple register in the archive of knowing (see Guha 1999, Amin 1995, Pandey 2001).

In conclusion, tortured prisoners' bodies became the location of a political project surrounded by secrecy and the political power of fictive character. Secrecy and fiction, embodied in violent rituals, and molding their characteristics, continue to be a part of Mukls' lives even today. Mukls' files in the StB archive, produced during the early stages of violence, are the evidence that allow us to see the formation of fictive political power.

Interrogation was a continuing and reinforcing experience for many Mukls during imprisonment and even after release. Mukls' new subjectivity was shaped by many factors. One was their immediate invisibility and denial of family life and kinship relatedness after arrest and during interrogations. Alienation as they recall, through the strong sense of their own interiority, voice, and agency, they experienced the power of kin relatedness.

The question they often ask themselves when they speak about the interrogations and torture is "Our own people put us through this hell; why is no one now held responsible?" These questions remain in individual narratives, and in conversation when Mukls gather as a group. In many cases their understanding of state political power and their relationships to their torturers was based on their consciousness of the temporal character of the totalitarian state's political power. Yet they often speak about tragedy, the damaging events that should not have happened, inflicted by human action, from which they bear the injustice. If this book should be characterized as an ethnography of cruelty, then I hope to show that the practice of cruelty through different modes of subjectivization has, in various forms, agency as well as tragic continuity for the Mukls and their families.

The Communist Party produced, by simulation of death and then rebirth, a new subject, a Mukl, less than human in the mind of the party and its sympathizers, but ironically a free agent according to some surviving Mukls.

NOTES

1. See Guha 1999, and Amin 1995.

2. Pankrác was a prison in Prague, where political prisoners were held after arrest until their trials.

3. See *Uranový Gulag: Jáchymovské peklo* by Zdeněk Šedivý (2003).

4. Leopoldov prison in Leopoldov, Slovakia, is a seventeenth-century fortress built as protection from the Ottoman Turks. In the nineteenth century the fort was converted into a high-security prison. Once the largest prison in Hungary, in the twentieth century it became housing for political prisoners.

5. This narrative is included to demonstrate the extensive remembering of the humiliation of others. In general, Mukls' narration tends to be less linear. Compared to other testimony, Dr. K's was one of the most articulated. His narratives seem to be organized and he was not emotional, as some of the others were when they spoke of their own experience of torture. Only later did I learn that his story was published as a biography (Bednářová 2000). Some among the Mukls and Muklyněs I have interviewed had published their stories in the form of biographies or autobiographies after 1989. Written narratives were often more self-directed than interviews. They seemed to write more openly about interrogations and torture than speaking about them during their interviews.

6. See *V Zúženém Prostoru* by Václav Černý (1994) and *Osmašedesátý* by Petr Pithart (1990).

Chapter Four

Trial

The Show Trial was the judicial event during which, by law, the political others lost their social face and citizenship in the public eye. "Who is not with us is against us," was a common Communist slogan in 1948 Czechoslovakia. During the first year of Communist political power, led by the first Communist president, Klement Gottwald, the party's focus was on the liquidation of any imagined enemy of the new People's Democratic Republic (*Lidová Demokratická Republika*) (see Feierabend 1988). The Show Trials were group trials during which men and women were forced by the state into the courtroom. On the stage in the courtroom they were accused of homeland betrayal. For Mukls the trials became one of the most recognized public humiliations of all political events of the 1950s in Czechoslovakia. The trial event was the final stage of a Mukl's passage in the process of becoming a criminal. The trials emerge as critical historical events during which "the lived space of time is altered" (Trnka 2008:14).

The trials, in contrast to the arrests and interrogations, were made public. The Show Trial, legally constructed political theater, was performed for the audience selected by the state and broadcast by radio for the masses. The ruling interest group promoted its will, and law in Czechoslovakia became "authoritarian law" (Pospisil 1971). The Communist state used the law to demonstrate its political power and to spread fear. The new legal order supported the state's political fiction. For Mukls, the law became a symbol of their public shame, their public defacement.

In this section I look at political events, the trials, and examine how law was used during the Show Trials in 1950's Czechoslovakia. I will discuss ways in which the judicial system took part in the political theater and disciplined political others by forcing them to perform acts of self-accusation. I demonstrate how Mukls' declarations of their estrangement from the legal order are linked to their alienation from the state or nation. To show this, I will expand on the concepts of defacement, fictional political power, and Mukls' memories of humiliation. I will discuss these themes in the context of the courtroom, where Mukls' experiences were displayed, exposed and made public. I suggest, in this chapter, that violent historical processes in the 1950s in Czechoslovakia not only shaped the judicial system, but also laid the groundwork for new cultural patterns under socialism, which persisted even after its collapse.

Based on the assumption that the modern state and the law are inseparable, in the Weberian tradition, I draw from anthropological works concerned with law, violence and change in modern state societies. In particular, I refer to the work of Talal Asad, Veena Das, Deborah Poole, Leopold Pospisil, Susanna Trnka, and Jared Zigon. When engaging with my own data, I found the critical approach to legal studies utilized by the scholars Bernard S. Cohen, Joan Vincent, Francis G. Snyder, Laura Nader, Carol Greenhouse, and Lawrence Rosen helpful. Their concern with political power and constructions of legal change proved especially helpful. Further, my analysis is shaped by Giorgio Agamben's philosophy of sovereignty (Agamben 2000) and Hannah Arendt's political philosophy of the totalitarian state (Arendt 1966). In reference to Muklhood, the important question is not how the law reflects culture, but rather how law is reconstituted and how it can be a defining feature of newly developing cultural patterns.

POLITICAL THEATER AND CITIZENS ON TRIAL

The first Show Trials began after president Gottwald returned from Moscow. As part of the follow-up to his conversations with Stalin (Kaplan 1989), Gottwald signed many life imprisonment or death sentences. Directed liquidation of the former political elite, members of the pre–World War II political parties, expanded to the elimination of anybody acting, or suspected of acting, against Soviet-like political and economic reforms. Thus state nationalization of private properties, from small family businesses to large factories, schools, hospitals, farmlands, and forests, became a process during which citizens suspected by the regime of being enemies were killed or sentenced to prison. Soviet power was distributed on two levels: ideological and material.[1] "The February victory of working classes" (Tigrid 1982) became part of Stalin's plan to "mobilize European Communists" (Táborský 1970), and, in the name of this plan, Czech Communists were directed to speed up the process leading towards a dictatorship of the proletariat. The Communist Party (with a majority of votes) moved to eliminate the power of the remaining political parties.

In the fall of 1948, Soviet *Rajcin comandos* from the KGB arrived in Prague to assist with the process of interrogations before the Monster Trials (see Rupnik 2002). Historical trials, in the 1950s in Czechoslovakia, are known collectively as the Monster Trials or Show Trials. Prior to the arrival of the *comandos*, the Soviet Army had occupied Czechoslovakia since 1945.[2] The Communist, Stalinist, revolution in Czechoslovakia was the starting point for the rebuilding of a new modern, socialistic state. Post-revolutionary Czechoslovakian Communist governments developed political and economic plans for realization of the socialist project. This project turned into a long-term process during which state violence became a tool for the maintenance of dominance and disciplinary power. Radical Socialist and Soviet political forces and actors were confronted by organized underground political parties and by individuals opposed to the practices of the Communist regime in Czechoslovakia. This opposition was suppressed. The political others became legal enemies of the state.

The Communist Parliament approved two new laws: 231/1948, Betrayal of and Espionage against the Peoples' Democratic Republic (10.24 1948), and 247/1948, A Law Creating Forced Labor Camps (10.25 1948).[3] These two new laws allowed the Communist Party to justify the liquidation[4] of the political others denounced publicly as enemies. It also established new ethical codes to be utilized for social domination. Paragraph 231 became, among the Mukls, not only a symbol of totalitarian sovereign power but also the symbol of judicial failure to protect its citizens. More importantly, Mukls also saw the law as a moral failure.

In 1948 the judicial institution was the transmitter of political power. The life of law, *zákon* (*lex*, in Latin), in an abstract sense, and in its implied principles, *právo* (*ius*, in Latin), was changed to "authoritarian law" (Pospisil 1971) and imposed upon the Czechoslovak population against its will. The courtroom became a place for the final performance of a highly emotional, psychological and political play. The script was written in advance and well rehearsed during months of interrogations. The law represented the political ideology. The judge, the prosecution and the defense acted in the interest of the state. Staged Monster Trials were visible confirmations of the Czechoslovak Communist government's subordination to Soviet political power in Central Europe.

Several of the Trials became famous, for example, the trials of Rudolf Slánský and Milada Horáková.[5] During the Slánský trial in 1952, in which members of the Communist Party were involved, the performative character of the trials reached its highest point. Slánský, second in rank to president Gottwald, was a major player on the Czechoslovakian political scene in the 1950s. Based on historical documents, he was involved in sentencing enemies of the party to death. Ironically, Slánský was arrested, interrogated under Soviet supervision, and put on trial along with thirteen other leading Czech Communists. The confession was central to these events. When interrogated, prisoners were forced to rehearse confessions for the trial. One of the survivors from this group, Edward Goldstucker, remembered: "The key was confession, after that proof was not needed at all" (Justmanová 2000). Slánský and others from the group were accused of high treason and espionage, of being Trotskyites and Zionists, and of preparing an anti-Communist revolt. They publicly accused themselves of crimes against the Czechoslovak state. This trial ended the lives of eleven prisoners. The Slánský trial is described in detail by one of the three survivors, Artur London, who wrote about his own trial: "I rehearsed my long lecture without interruption. I said my text with coldness, carefully, like it is not about me. I had the feeling as if it is not about me, that I am involved only as a witness of the interrogation of my doppelganger" (London 1968:301). The Show Trials represent a political and personal tragedy of this time and illuminate Soviet political interests in Europe, Israel and other regions after World War II.

Jana Svehlova pointed out the problematic position of children of arrested members of the Communist Party, many of whom were Jews, whose parents were part of some of the famous trials.[6] (While I think this is a very important subject, because of a lack of research data, I cannot pursue this analysis any further. However, later in this book, I address Mukls' and their kin's diversity, fragmentation and reconciliation.) In many ways the Mukls' story is not homogeneous. Deeper investigation reveals different individual experiences based on personal histories. In my investigation I do not specifically discuss diversity along ethnic or religious lines, but I do emphasize the diversity of Muklhood, as well as shared patterns.

The trial of Milada Horáková was different. She was a survivor of several Nazi prisons and an active opponent of the Communist Party. Horáková, a member of the National Democratic Socialist Party and a member of the Czechoslovak Parliament, was also the first woman to receive the death sentence during this period.[7] Along with Horáková, 650 people were arrested, 639 were tried in sixty-three groups, and ten people were executed. The trial of Horáková became an important symbol in multiple ways. For the state, it was a chance to show its power. By accusing these women, Milada Horáková, Františka Zemínková, and Antonie Kleinerová, as leaders of the insurgency and giving them harsh punishments, the state strategically used women to shock the resistance by its level of cruelty. Horáková was executed; Zemínková and Kleinerová were sentenced to life in prison. The state used these women, put them on trial, to discipline others in the resistance and to empower the workers and the Communist Party.

The atmosphere in the courtrooms was intense. One of the prisoners on trial remembered: "I was waiting for the final verdict in fear, then the judge announced my life sentence, and I was feeling joy. I remember my desire to sing the national anthem, but the audience in the courtroom was screaming for harsher punishment, and so I didn't sing" (National Film Archive 2005). Horáková's trial was broadcast live on Czechoslovak Radio and filmed. In villages and towns the radio broadcast was connected to outdoor speakers. Documentary films, now in the National Film Archive show workers' demonstrations at the time of the trials. The individual speakers at these demonstrations were calling for punishment and offering hours of free labor in exchange for harsher punishments for those on trial (National Film Archive 2005).[8]

Mukl Franta remarked: "She was an active player on the political scene, but not well known among the larger population, until the trial when she acted firmly and strongly until the end." Horáková's last words in the courtroom were: "I insist on my beliefs, for I support my position and information based on the authority of two Czechoslovak presidents, T. G. Masaryk, and Eduard Beneš, who were influential on my life" (Dvořáková 2001:56). According to witnesses, she defended her innocence with courage and showed no sense of fear. Mukls find power and admiration for her political ethics in the context of her life. She was a professional woman involved in the practice of law, a politician, an active feminist and a family person. She survived Nazi torture, but not the Communist regime. For Mukls she is a heroine. In Czechoslovak history she was the first woman victim of the Monster Trials who was visible to the public.

Milada Horáková's last words before her execution became a powerful symbol of this political period: "Padám, padám . . . tento boj jsem prohrála, odcházím čestně, miluji tuto zemi, miluji tento lid—budujte mu blahobyt. Odcházím bez nenávisti k vám a přeji vám. . . ." She did not finish, she choked on the rope. It was 5:30 a.m., July 27, 1950 (Lesák 2000). In English: "I am falling out, falling down . . . I lost this fight, I am leaving with pride, I love this country, I love its people—develop prosperity for them. I am leaving without hatred toward you and wish you . . . (author's translation)." In her last words we can read Horáková's determination to face the state and its judicial system without fear, regret or bitterness. She had a charismatic personality and was exceptionally strong in her resistance to the fictive power of the state. Mukls and also other Czechs and Slovaks remember her courage as an important symbol of the political resistance in the 1950s. Her sympathizers, among them many Mukls, formed a new organization named after her, the Club of Milada Horáková.

In June 2004, I attended one of their annual memorial gatherings to mark Horáková's execution. The gathering was organized in two locations, Pankrác prison, the place of her execution, and in the National Cemetery in Vyšehrad, her symbolic burial place.[9] The ceremony at Pankrác was a deeply emotional experience. A small group of club members gathered in front of the prison entrance. We passed through several gates and walked into the prison courtyard. In our conversation Mukls remembered this space from the 1950s. I knew some of these memories from their individual life narratives: the memory of mothers nursing their newborn babies under the gallows, Christmas time memories, memories of sounds they made when communicating from cell to cell, and above all the memories of the suffering of others. Pankrác prison is designed, as prisons are, to police and punish, and it leaves visitors with a sense of desolation in its gray and bare space. The actual ceremony, a speech and the national anthem, took place on the east side of Pankrác prison, hidden away in the corner by the wall where Horáková was executed.

The philosopher Agamben in his writing on camps explored the link between the state and judicial structures. Agamben's writing on camps is relevant for me because of the connection he makes between law and citizenship. Agamben discussed this using the example of the camp at Dachau, opened for political prisoners by the Nazi regime in Germany (see 2000:38–39). He writes, "The camp is the space that opens up when the state of exception starts to become the rule" (Agamben 2000:38). Such a state of exception requires the temporal absence of state law. "It is only because the camps constitute a space of exception—a space in which the law is completely suspended—that everything is truly possible in them" (Agamben 2000:40).

There were many fewer famous trials experienced by lesser-known people than Horáková or Slánský. Most men and women did not become national heroes, and many, even without trial, were sentenced to work camps for life.

For a Mukl or Muklyně, the remembering of the trial is the memory of the space of death. The courtroom experience was a unique time during their passage. The interrogator's task of preparing prisoners for their trials was connected to the idea of defacement. The goal was to convince the prisoner to perform the speech act during which one admits the shame of his betrayal of the People's Republic. Veena Das spoke of a "zone between two deaths" (Das and Kleinman 2000) as a place of temporal death, from which the voice of a witness to a crime can speak an otherwise unspeakable truth about the criminality of law. Each trial lasted several hours, some even days. It was a time of double register, when the Mukl's face was unveiled to the public, exposed from secrecy, and at the same time shamed, defaced. In the courtroom, the prosecutor's speech, legal texts, written laws, the language of judges and even defense lawyers were used by the government to establish legitimate reasons for the liquidation of the political other and the creation of new, public notions of fear. The Mukls were publicly, under judicial approbation, excluded from the nation or state. The trial legalized the final exclusion by degrading

Mukls as criminals. They lost dignity in the eyes of the public. Causing the political other to lose face within the community became an intentional act of defacement by the totalitarian state and carried out through the justice system.

Trial, like arrest and interrogation, was a frequent point of reference in Mukls' narratives. Those who had to pass through the courtroom and were marked as enemies of the Peoples' Republic remembered the trials:

> **Albína:** We were allowed to ask for nice clothes from home and to fix our hair, so that we would convince the public during the trial that pre-trial prison had not taken away our human dignity. Particularly, the family was supposed to leave the courtroom convinced that their relatives were cared for. I refused different clothes and went to my trial in the skirt I wore all those months after arrest.

> **Hilda:** Before the trial they added medications to our food and coffee, causing a weakness of our will, so that we would say what they wanted at the trial. They didn't succeed, because we were filled with hate and felt misjudged. I was active (a partisan) during the protectorate and after the war I received a medal. My father brought it to the courtroom and the judge dismissed it. He said that I was tricky during the protectorate, and I am tricky now as well.

Many remembered clearly, just like Albína and Hilda, the time before the trial. After the months of interrogations, a Mukl was prepared for trial. Many refused to cooperate, and many were so traumatized that preparations aimed at masking their degradation and pain failed. Jiří K could not remember his trial well:

> I was so brainwashed I don't remember. I know it only from listening to memories of others about the staged, tragic comedy in the courtrooms. The judicial language of the prosecutor was full of jargon, every second word was "imperialist agent" and some words they took directly from Russian, like *narušitelé* (disturbers). In my group were tried with me farmers who helped a number of people over the border, but then also some Prague criminals.

Jiří's fragmented memory denied him a return to the time of his suffering. The failure of a traumatized memory is the result of physical and psychological pain. This form of suffering has been well documented in various ethnographic accounts, particularly in two edited series on social suffering and violence and subjectivity (Das, Kleinman, Lock, Ramphele, and Reynolds 2001, and Das, Kleinman, Ramphele, and Reynolds 2000; Kleinman, Das, and Lock 1997). In their accounts of how the collective experience of violence can alter individual subjectivity, scholars of violence show how social force transforms itself into political violence. Ethnographic investigations of violent acts and their impact on everydayness are based on the processes through which violence is actualized; that is, the violence is examined not only as production but also as consumption (Das 2007). These scholars argue, too, that whether violence is seen "as a remnant of long standing primordial conflict" (Das and Kleinman 2000:1) or classified as "a sign of the distortion of focal moral worlds by forces (national or global) which originate outside of those worlds and over which local communities can exercise little control" (Das and Kleinman 2000:1), it is necessary to consider *the formation of the subject position.*

The state assumed that the Mukls' passage through interrogations prepared them for the trials. The Mukl was expected to publicly acknowledge his or her guilt for crimes against the state or government, which identified itself with the nation, the country, and the people. For the state, the Monster Trial was a publicly staged ritual marking the criminal act. In the courtroom the judge, prosecutors and defense attorneys were loyal state employees, paid to accuse the political other of the crime of betrayal of the state or nation. Václav Vaško in his autobiography described the trial:

> The day of the trial I woke up feeling like a soldier before a battle. They loaned me my clothes that I had on when I was arrested. On the bench of the prosecuted were (six names) and in between us the guards. In walked the judge, two members of the trial committee and a secretary. After a formal opening the representative of the state justice department, Kudrna, read the accusations. It was an extensive construct of lies and half-truths ending with words suggesting that the goal of the organization of Catholic groups was to create groups of religious members, whose religious beliefs were planned to be misused to agitate for dissatisfaction with the Peoples' Democratic Regime and in the final stage to prepare for the overthrow of this regime, which all these accused people knew about and they organized themselves to destroy the Peoples' Democratic State and its order, secured by the constitution. (Vaško 1999:179)

While being subjected to arrest and interrogation alienated Mukls from their families and communities, for the state the trial had the effect and purpose of excluding the Mukls from the nation and the state. Without exception every Mukl mentioned the trial, but only some discussed it in detail. According to the Mukls, each trial differed based on specific circumstances: the members of the accused group, the prosecutor and the judge. In some cases prisoners were allowed to try to defend themselves; in other cases they were not.

Julia recalls, "The verdicts were prearranged by the secret police, my lawyer was assigned to me by State Police. He didn't help me at all and I received 15 years for espionage" (Bouška and Pinerová 2009:43). Jiří K could/ would not remember his trial well, but he remembered his sentence and the sentences of those on trial with him.

Imprisoned in many prisons and after one year of continuous interrogations we were condemned to high punishment. From our group six people got the death sentence and one of them was executed. Five of them had their sentences changed to twenty-five or thirty years in prison. From this we served many years, I myself eight, and others ten years. After returning from prison the persecutions continued.

A political prisoner was expected to perform; that is, confess to the act of betrayal, based on the state's script. Judges who acted in conformity with totalitarian power by mechanically ordering political uniformity using legal processes performed the Monster Trials. One of the Mukls remembered:

> They requested that one would repeat the statement from the interrogation. I was not shy and I argued with the judge about Communist ideology. The funniest thing was that those idiots were broadcasting our trial live on loud speakers. My sentence was eleven years for high treason and spying.

The state used the media to reach a larger audience and to expand its influence outside of the courtroom. The Trials were broadcast by loudspeaker in big cities as well as small towns and villages. The media disseminated fictive criminalization throughout the country and thereby secured the political geography of the state. Many Mukls and their relatives spoke about the government's poisonous intentions and its aim to provoke public hatred towards Mukls. This resulted in a wave of hatred towards political others. Individuals began to fear that they would become politically polluted by any connection to a political other.

Linda Vlasák, who fled Czechoslovakia in 1948, said this to me.

> The people in the small Canadian town couldn't imagine why we left Czechoslovakia in 1948. They questioned: What have you done that you had to leave? When we were marked for persecution we were proud. My mother was stripped by Communists of dignity, she was abused by her own community. They took her law office away and made her work as a lowest helper. The people from the community in her town who used to come to her for help, all of a sudden crossed the street when they saw her coming down the sidewalk. Her sorrow was over the weakness of her own people who betrayed her. If not there, where else can you look?

It was this sense of betrayal by countrymen, more than by government, that was intensely painful to those who were persecuted or arrested. Party functionaries decided on the verdicts, signed them before the trial and passed them on to the judges. What followed were reenactments of judicial processes. In the courts, Show Trials turned into symbolic political theater intended to legitimatize the state's oppressive acts. In some cases prisoners were tried in alternative spaces to courtrooms. Muklyně Květa testified in her interview, recorded by Tomaš Bouška and Klára Pinerová:

> The trial was in a local public house, some place where theater plays used to be put on. We were on the stage and all the people of the village were sitting in the audience. I remember Holec declaring: "Ladies and gentleman this is not a trial this is a theatre play." My uncle had his trial in Kutná Hora in Tyl's theatre. (Bouška and Pinerová 2009:62)

Olga remembered the audience: "The courtroom was full of a forced audience, workers, and students. They called us one after the other. My mother got twenty-two years, my father ten, and I fifteen, but I for doing nothing. I didn't participate in anything."

The audiences in the courtroom were party members who bought tickets. With some exceptions, the family members of the accused were not allowed to be in the courtroom. By the time the prisoners were called to the courtroom, they were exhausted, and whether they recited the official accusation or not, the prisoners were found guilty by the state-appointed lawyers and judges of acts against the Peoples' Republic. Mukl Zdeněk remembered in the interview:

> On March 14th and 15th in 1951 we stood in front of the court. It was a Monster process. It was a public process and they invited all the young students from the schools and young people from factories. It was in the courtroom in Hradec and we were judged as a dangerous and frightening case to society. Accused of high treason, espionage and other crimes, our group was sentenced to anywhere from 14 years to 1 year in prison.

The prisoner at the trial lost the face of a loyal citizen and was marked by the state as a criminal. The trial became a judicial event that evoked defacement. The political others, by law, lost their social face in the public eye. Mukls spoke in their narratives about the state's intention to create their public shame. Courtrooms became the stages of a political project in its most extreme. Mukls were criminalized for their political otherness under newly enacted Communist state laws. The accusations were initiated by the state secret police and punishments ratified by the judicial institutions.

Among the arrested were different people with diverse backgrounds. Albína in her narratives remembered:

> I noticed that among those arrested was a small percentage of women from circles affected the most by the regime: business people, factory owners, wealthy families with traditions and big names. In prison I met with few exceptions,

women from lower backgrounds—secretaries, teachers, saleswomen, women from farms, factories, housewives and students. None of these women owned property that could be nationalized, and they still resisted against the state, because they felt the injustice imposed on our citizens. They fought for the ideal. They fought for the ones who lost it all.

From Albína's testimonies about different types of prisoners, we can see the extent of the political fiction of the state in relation to the judicial system and its effect on Czechoslovaks. The law failed to protect its citizens, including some of those favored by the state. Paradoxically, the state, which claimed to conform to a socialistic workers' revolution, eventually turned against the workers themselves. This historical irony was discussed by several historians (Kaplan 1989, Rupnik 2002, Táborský 1970, Tigrid 1982) and is one of the central themes of those writing about organized violence in Central and Eastern Europe (Havel 1989, Kundera 1967, Škvorecký 1990). The men and women from factories who were, early on, recruited as an audience to call "hang them" were later targeted themselves. Law, order and justice as reconstructed by the Communist Party in Czechoslovakia were sufficient instruments for the governmental liquidation of the political other. Individual prisoners were called to admit their own betrayal of the Peoples' Republic. The principles of law aligned with the Communists' ideology lost their dimension for justice, and the courtroom became a performative stage directed by the state.

Anežka gave two reasons for her arrest and sentence. She and her husband owned a private business and also knew soldiers who fought at Dukla, the place of a significant defeat of the German Nazi Army by the Soviet Red Army. Anežka revealed that she and her husband had agreed that if they were arrested she would take the blame on herself.

> They charged us under paragraph 231 for betrayal and espionage. We did everything so that at least one of us will get out of it. He got four years and I received twenty-two.
>
> Somebody revealed that we were active against the Nazis and that made it harder for us. I didn't see my husband until the trial on the 21st of January 1951. A whole group was taken to the courtroom and then they read testimonies individually. I recognized only my husband and a cousin from the group. I could barely recognize my husband; they did treat the men much worse. It was terrible. The judge was a Slovak, a terrible monster. We had a public defender, but he didn't say a word at the trial. Our children gave him a lot of money.

Former soldiers and freedom fighters were considered the most dangerous by the Soviet political powers. Professional soldiers, who fought against Nazism on the western or eastern fronts, became, after the war, one of the regime's first targets of terror. According to some Mukls, they received the longest sentences to prison camps.[10] Mukls, like Anežka, tried with an army group would also receive longer sentences.

The soldiers' mindset is, for example, revealed in the story of the Mašin brothers (Němeček 1998). It is evident from the Mašins' testimony, and from Mukls I have interviewed, that some who were active in the resistance movement during World War II, and had an opportunity to observe the political discourse after the war, continued fighting for their homeland on some level. The professional soldiers formed a separate group within the Mukls' confederation. One of their annual memorials is organized every year on the date when General Pika was executed. Pika's case became a symbol of resistance within the army. For professional soldiers the punishments were some of the most severe. One of the professional soldiers I interviewed, Rudolf, remembered Pika's trial:

> I was part of Pika's group trial. I was given twenty years of heavy prison, from that I "sat" eleven and a half. I was in different prisons and for seven years I worked in the uranium mines. Immediately after the trial I was sent to the prison in Bory (Plzeň). I was kept in isolation.

Anežka's memory of her husband in the courtroom is typical of many who saw someone they knew on trial. The secrecy surrounding this violence was ruptured during the trial but was to be ongoing in the camps. Some Mukls saw their relatives in the courtroom after months of knowing nothing about them. After the trial they again lost them. Many, like Anežka, could see that their relatives or friends were changed. During imprisonment many Mukls lost weight or were injured. The recognition of the suffering, which took place before the trial, stripped away the secrecy and produced painful knowledge in the courtroom.

Anežka, and also others, spoke of Law 231. Law 231, crafted by the state in 1948 to maintain its political power, became for the prisoners a concrete symbol of normalized state violence; the law secured the normalization of violent practices. It was on the basis of this law that all the Mukls were tried. Law 231 became a symbol of judicial failure to protect the nation's citizens. It also showed how the strategy for state ideology could be channeled through the courtroom; a Mukl on trial was accused of betrayal under Law 231. In the clash between the state leaders' imagined Peoples' Republic and Mukls' sense of homeland, the new state had won.

As I closely examined Mukls' memories of legal state performances, I agreed with Victor Turner that "social dramas have the habit of activating classificatory oppositions which may be outside of traditional social divisions and turn them into conflict" (Turner 1969: 10). For Turner, social life is rich with social drama; he argues that legal, just as theatrical or ritualistic performance, generates relevation of experience. Judicial process, according to him, just like ritual process, nearly always represents a transition from one social form to another. In my own work, transformative action applies to the notion of belonging. The Mukls' sense of belonging to their homeland was turned upside down during the trial. Their own people, the ones now governing their homeland, publicly marked them at the trial as criminals. Accused as a betrayer, the Mukl felt betrayed by his people and his government. The formation of violence within the interior of the state became, for the political actor, a rite of passage. Arendt emphasized the intentional dehumanization of citizens who are subjected to state-produced violent rituals (Arendt 1966:592). She offered a political-ethical analysis of Stalinism, different in its analytical nature from Solzhenitsyn's, but also emphasizing the character of totalitarian political power. She differentiated the totalitarian form of a political system as one that is built on the assumption that everything is possible.

The rhythm of what Allen Feldman identifies as "simulations of death," "restoration of time," and "transformational movement of the political actor through the interior of the state" (Feldman 1991:137) makes this political act, the trial, a rite of passage. Violent ritual is understood here as the transitional passage through repetitive political terror. For Mukls, the cumulative experience of arrest, interrogations and trial is more than a sequence of events, it is "the transitional passage through the repetitive political terror" (Feldman 2001:86). The rite of passage in that experience of closeness to death becomes a transformative experience. The transformation of the Mukls' sense of belonging, from alienation to exclusion, was a no-less-traumatic moment than arrest or interrogation. In this sense the performative political efforts acomplished their aim, which was to secretly and publicly transform citizens into Mukls and Muklynĕs.

The trial was both an experiencial event and a symbolic one. The politics of state were expressed through the trial as ritualized drama, "the statement in action" (Leach 1964). Just like drama, the trial perfomance not only defined the roles for actors but was also charged with emotions. The symbolic meaning of this drama communicates power relations to the audience in the courtroom and through the media, by means of radio and loudspeakers located in public places throughout the country, to people outside. The political fiction and legitimized power of leaders, in Émile Durkheim's sense, was during the trial, socially approved. This symbolized a new relationship between individual and group. The ritualized trials controlled the process, and as Victor Turner put it, "Retribalization, whether defined as fascism, socialism, communism, or any other mode of authoritarian or totalistic control, must seek to control crises of all types not only by force but also by reritualization of the third phase of all social drama" (Turner 1969:112).

DEFACEMENT AND KINSHIP

The Mukls' story is the story of citizens rejected by their own Czechoslovakian community. Their traumatic and painful experiences are deeply rooted in the knowledge of their own people's accusations of betrayal during the Monster Trials. The subject of pain is one of the main themes in this book. The experience of pain, woven into Mukls' rites of passage proved to be critical for the formation of their subjectivities. Earlier I emphasized the role of kinship during the time of arrests and interrogations. I examined how kinship became a mechanism of punishment, one form of the state's inflictions of the pain on prisoners. In this section, I will discuss further the Mukls' pain as it was shared with their families during the Show Trials. When remembering their trials, Mukls remembered that their families were not allowed to be in the courtroom.

> **Albína:** The trial was supposed to last two days. Upon entering the courtroom my eyes spotted the audience behind the bars. My father wasn't there and I felt relieved. My father will be protected from the humiliating form the trial took. As a lawyer, he would not handle it well. In many instances family were not allowed in the courtroom and had to wait outside in the hallway.

> **Hana:** Our trial was open to the members of our families. I could see my mother, my father and my future husband's parents. There were eleven of us on trial, but I was the only woman. Our group got 15–13 years . . . after the trial they took us underground, I looked back at my father and people I knew. The police officer told me off doing that. I said, "I will always be part of my family whenever and wherever." He reported me and I was punished the next day. (Bouška and Pinerová 2009:89)

> **Dagmar:** On the benches were sitting the ones whose lives were on trial, and in the hallways the families waited silently in fear. They waited for the moment they could see the faces of mothers, fathers, brothers and sisters, and for many this was the last moment, because they were not allowed to see them before the death penalty or they were told: Madam, they have already hung him, go home and don't make theater here. (Šimková 1994:73).

In their recollections of their trials, Mukls, or their kin, spoke about their mutual connectedness and shared pain. The secrecy surrounding pre-trial imprisonment made it impossible for relatives of the arrested to know what was done to prisoners and where they were being held. They came to the courtroom, if allowed, to witness the pain of their kin who were lost in time. From their perspective, arrested mothers, fathers, and siblings were transformed by torture; their experiences were unimaginable. Some testified that their relatives on trial were hard to recognize after the months of torture. They spoke about Mukls' facial changes, loss of body weight and crushed spirit. Some Mukls were unable to speak during their trial, but some did speak. One of the daughters, Daniela, remembered the courtroom.

For 13 months, no officials answered our questions about the whereabouts of our father, why they took him away, and was he alive? Without any news and with fear about daddy's life, we suddenly received permission to attend his trial that was to take place in another town, Uherské Hradiště. The show that the judges presented was shocking. The individuals struggling into the courtroom were human wrecks. Some of the prisoners had to be supported to walk, others walked with crutches. We screamed with horror when we saw them. The judge was banging the table with his fist and yelled at us that we would be thrown out if we were not quiet. There were many workers from factories and the hall was completely full. I felt sorry for my father, first and foremost, but he wasn't afraid. We just didn't want to play the inferior and the humiliated.

The trial testimonies reveal that Mukls' pain and humiliation was paralyzing and deeply traumatic. In the public light of trial, Mukls' own sense of reality crystallized after months of uncertain disorientation. The trial was the painful final revelation of exclusion from the public space for Mukls and final separation from their kin. Death sentences or life in prison were the usual outcomes. The state, by criminalizing the political other through the judicial system, was able, legally and physically, to exclude some of its citizens from any function in society. It is this different way of belonging or being excluded that distinguished the state and its political others. For all political others their trial was an intensive moment in their passage, remembered as a traumatic and painful separation between oneself and the state.

Mukls' alienation from the nation or state in the act of public defacement during the trial altered their sense of public voice. Mukls were judicially excluded from public space, so it was only on the stage of the courtroom that their pain became visible to their kin. The trial reshaped Mukls' kinship through witnessing pain. After their loss of belonging to the state, Mukls lost their public ground. Kinship then, from their perspective, was their only available place of belonging, their private ground. Ironically, though, kinship ties continued to change after the trial. Mukls' memories from labor camps and prisons show us the shifting nature of their kinship ties. There, in the camps and prisons, Mukls' sense of belonging was transformed into a new social context.

JUDICIAL FICTION AND DOUBLE FACE

The idea of belonging to the nation or state was at the very center of the political clash in Czechoslovakia during the early 1950s. Ruptured relations between citizens and the state had consequences. While the state used the judicial system for its ideological interests, the political other on trial felt betrayed by that same judicial system as it subverted the practice of law.

Leopold Pospisil reminds us of the cultural expectations of the law in Czechoslovakia, when he wrote that people were "accustomed to regard the law of the state as the primary standard to which the individual looks for protection and with which he tries to conform in his behavior" (Pospisil 1971). For Mukls, law was not just a framework of basic conformity, but the constitution for morality. During their group conversations, Mukls often referred to new Communist laws as immoral anti-laws (Pospisil 1971). Ironically, the language of the new laws, 231/1948 and 247/1948, conveyed the register of morality, but promoted the interest of the state's ideology and accused political others of immorality against the people's republic. The legal language was constructed to shame citizens for their politics, which were different from state politics. In the Mukls' view, the immorality of the law materialized itself in newly written legal documents and in the construction of judicial lies serving Soviet political interests.

Arendt, in her discussion of totalitarian organization, saw the role of the totalitarian ruler as a dual and contradictory one. "He must establish the fictitious world of the movement as a tangible working reality of everyday life, and he must, on the other hand, prevent this new world from developing a new stability; for a stabilization of its laws and institutions would surely liquidate the movement itself and with it the hope for eventual world conquest" (Arendt 1996:391). Maintaining the rules of a fictitious world was essential for the maintenance of totalitarian power in Communist Czechoslovakia. For Arendt, that kind of power is in direct confrontation with reality. As a result, totalitarianism "is constantly concerned with overcoming this challenge" (Arendt 1995:392). According to Arendt, totalitarianism in power uses the state's administration for two purposes: long-term world conquest and domestic experiments in transforming reality into fiction.

In his memoir Radim Kuthan published the official legal text of the accusation against him:

The state court in Prague is accusing (66 names) that from the spring of 1948 until January 1949 in Prague they:

1. conducted an attempted liquidation of the Peoples' Democratic regime and the social and economic structure of the republic, secured by the constitution, and forcefully interrupted constitutional activity of the president of the republic, the congress and the parliament.
2. committed espionage of state secret matters with the intention of passing information to foreign powers.
3. for the conduct of evil doing listed above in I committed/attempted holding of means to which contributed to its realization.

4. after acquiring the information about the criminal acts in I did not report such to the safety bureau office.

5. held in secrecy from investigators rank, which could help in discovering the criminal. They intentionally were covered and hid criminals from immediate superiors, which leads to their criminal act of betrayal, espionage, covering up of a criminal act, not reporting a criminal act, and will be punished according to law number 231/48. (Bubeníčková-Kuthanová 1991:33)

This is a translation of a legal document, legitimized by a court and on the basis of which Radim was sentenced to a labor camp. Mukls often made it a point to quote or read to me, during our conversations, literal legal formulation as evidence of how the state criminalized them. Judicially formulated accusations, such as this one, were typically prepared before the trial. When I spoke to Radim, he indicated that Judr. Čížek, a defense lawyer, visited him in prison one time before the trial. He told Radim: "For betrayal you will get something, but I will get you out of the spy accusation." Radim replied: "But Dr. Čížek, they are not accusing me of spying." "Even better," responded Čížek, and then he added: "It will be better if you just admit all of it." The judicial system and its pratitioners in Czechoslovakia played a significant role in transforming reality into fiction. Čeněk remembered his trial and death sentence as a continuous progression of events in the fall of 1949.

The investigating judge didn't come to me until a day before the trial. During the short meeting he said: "It looks bad and whatever you get don't protest, anything will be better than a death penalty." It was interesting for me, the judge was Chinese. He spoke Czech well, but with an accent. As I was waiting in one of the so-called death cells, I could hear when they were taking them for execution. Some were trying to kill themselves on the way. I could hear prisoners as they were hitting walls with their head. Some were silent, but in the end, before the execution all screamed for their mothers.

I was in fear of the idea that I could inflict pain on anybody outside. My consciousness confronted me about my choices and above all failing to protect my family. As I thought about my values, in contrast to hate and pain in surroundings, I was thinking a lot about the importance of the notion of love for life. I felt strongly that if I would maintain hate, I would shorten my life.

I was on trial in 1950. They called my mother and wife to come to the courtroom. I received the death penalty for political and army espionage against the socialist state. This was later changed to a life sentence with extra harsh conditions.

In his memory, Čeněk connected the fragments of his experiences into a continuous time line determined by fictive lies. When speaking, he tied arrest, interrogations, and trial together in such a way that I could see how the making of political fiction was embodied in all the events through which he had passed. He refused to refer to his experiences in terms of suffering, but rather in terms of living in a fictive condition in the space of death. I present Radim and Čeněk's testimonies to show two different ways Mukls remember this fictive character of the state politics ratified by judicial actions. For Radim, the fictive character of political power was located in the legal document constructed by the party and legalized by the courts. For Čeněk, the fiction was performed during the violent rituals, acted out in political theater, and identified by Mukls as a rite of passage taking them through the space of death. After trial the political other was sentenced to a camp for, in the legal language of the sentence, *převýchovu* (re-education); in the words of former camp guards, the sentence was for *likvidaci* (liquidation). The socialist state in 1948 Czechoslovakia transformed courtrooms into political theaters. The dramas, the trials and enactments of political fictions divided the state from its citizens who were placed on trial. In ritual ways the Show Trials defaced those individuals on the stage but unified them behind a new social mask— that of a Mukl. In this sense the trials were instrumental in establishing the dominance of the state's political fiction. Now political fiction, already part of the archive, was justified by courts of law.

Divisions between the state and its political others, finalized by the Show Trials, led to significant social and cultural changes. Show Trials resulted in the condition of dual face rooted in existential distinctions between the public and the private. They gave rise to what Václav Havel characterized as a time (1948–1989) in Czechoslovakia marked by "the multiple presence of the theme of human identity and existential schizophrenia" (Havel 1989:20). Lived dichotomy, public and private face, become accepted conditions of everyday existence. Havel defined this condition as a "moral crisis in society" (Havel 1989) and unique to life in a Communist state. Over time the Show Trials slowly poisoned the whole society to the point that duality of public and private face penetrated cultural patterns in significant ways. The duality of public and private face, forced on them by the state, was the only available condition in which Czech and Slovak people could exist. Finally, I suggest that over a longer period of time, general acceptance of the poisoned conditions, and adaptation to political fictions, became the norm and resulted in *Normalizace,* Normalization (this term refers to the period from 1968 to 1989). And so the political fiction of the 1950s was transformed after 1968 into political normality, and like the cancerous tumor it resembles, political violence spread into the whole body of society. The separation between public and private space became the norm and resulted in adaptation to a double-faced life; people in Czechoslovakia were socialized to lead double-faced lives. Even for those politically resisting individuals who claimed to be making individual moral choices, everyday life was double-faced. The concept of public face and private face was mainstreamed and worked into the cultural patterns of socialism. This double-faced life is one of the legacies of socialism.

CONCLUSION

Arrest, interrogation and trial proved to be critical events in Mukls' lives. I have identified the practices of the totalitarian political system in Czechoslovakia as a form of political power invested in those practices, which I conceptualize as violent rituals. The ritual as an analytical category opened the possibility for me to see Mukls' experiences, as felt by them as well as to identify the political expressions of the totalitarian state.

I argue that passage through a strategic state violent ritual, in particular, through the three stages of arrest, interrogation and trial, was an essential process in the formation of Mukls' subjectivity. I have discussed various modes of Mukls' subjectivity, including strategic social invisibility, alienation, political secrecy, fictive political power, public defacement, temporality and multiplicity of citizenship, political theater and judicial fiction, the politics of torture, the recall of humiliation and pain, and finally the moral and social duality of daily life. These modalities emerged as conceptual patterns from Mukls' narratives and become the framework for their story. I found that close investigation of Mukls' narratives about these events offers insight into what I see as essential aspects in the formation of their subjectivity, but also critical for an understanding of newly developed cultural patterns of politics and kinship.

I have argued that violent rituals transformed relatedness to kin and the state. For many, holding on to the old relatedness, along with new forms of relatedness, became a powerful means of survival. Relatedness opened up the possibility of passage through the violent state rituals, the space of death. The notion of lost face is a powerful expression for disappearance, criminalization, denial of family and citizenship, absence of legal justice, and above all the only available condition, that of bare life. The bare life is the only available condition when political others lived through torture and interrogations.

While examining social life through the political rituals, I discovered Mukls' strong sense of familial connectedness, as experienced through their pain. The shared pain phenomena, the Mukls' pain shared with their kin, is linked to newly developed distinctions between public and private space. In the Mukls' eyes the political force to which they were subjected is a criminal and immoral act, conducted by the state and approved by the justice system. I suggest that the traumatic experience of the violent events of the 1950s resulted in alienation, not just between the state and Mukls, but also between the state and its citizens in a larger sense. I argue that Mukls, Czechoslovakian political prisoners from 1948, who were publicly defaced and humiliated, were pushed out of a public space and into a space of political fiction. This fiction was dramatized and legitimized in the courtroom. For a Mukl and his kin this was an actual and traumatic experience; for the general audience this was political theater, highly charged symbolic performance. Further, these extraordinary events penetrated the daily lives of all citizens and poisoned society at large. The political trauma of the 1950s has left, to this day, a legacy of socialism in the Czech Republic and Slovakia.

> *Sometimes this violence is sudden, as in the dropping of the atomic bombs on Hiroshima and Nagasaki. At other times it takes the form of a continuous reign of terror, as with the policies and practices of the brutal regime of apartheid. Even when violence is not present in such dramatic forms, there can be the slow erosion of community through the soft knife of policies that severely disrupt the life worlds of people. And yet in the midst of the worst horrors, people continue to live, to survive, and to cope.*

—Das and Kleinman (2001)

NOTES

1. For example, the Soviets took over the Jáchymov uranium mines in September 1945 (Kroča 2003). According to Kroča, who wrote a short historical overview of Jáchymov mining, sixty men from the Soviet army occupied Jáchymov.

2. The liberation of Czechoslovakia by the Soviet army in 1945 turned into an occupation. Historians and documentary filmmakers have documented this historical moment. Mukls often testified about the Soviet presence in the camps. They also spoke about Soviet citizens and their children who were living in Prague in 1945 and were arrested by the KGB and sent to Siberia.

3. According to Kroča, the Communist government approved new laws very quickly. New prisoners were tried under these laws and sent to work camps as part of the solution to a shortage of labor. Kroča discusses this government act in the context of uranium mining (Kroča 2003).

4. Use of the term *liquidation* in Mukls' narratives varies. In many cases political actors in charge, such as guards and interrogators, used this term as a threat and an expression of power. In contrast to the Nazis' physical liquidation of Jews, Gypsies, or other groups, liquidation in the context of the Communist regime meant social death as well as biological death. The Communist aim was suppression of political and economic resistance. Opponents of the government were punished or in some instances, killed. The secrecy of the government's actions against its nonconformist citizens adds to the ambiguity of totalitarian political power in the Czech Republic.

5. Zuzana Justman presents this trial in the documentary film *A Trial in Prague.*

6. Documentation of these trials is in the Czech National Archive, Czech Film Archive in Prague, and available online on CT24 (Czech Television, channel 24).

7. For more on the this subject see www.enemysdaughters.com

8. Horáková's 1950 trial, held in Prague, lasted for seven hours. Her execution took place in Prague's Pankrác prison in June 1950. The Czech National Film Archive (NFA) released a five-and-a-half hour documentary film of this trial in 2005. For details of Horáková's life, see Dvořáková 2001.

9. Her cremated body was never found.

10. There was a Czechoslovak army in exile during WWII. The members of this army were trained professional soldiers from the pre-war Czechoslovak army or Czechoslovak volunteers trained in England. Units from the Czechoslovak army also fought on the eastern front. General Pika, one of those executed by the Communist regime in 1948, was commander of one of those units.

Part II

RECONCILIATION

Chapter Five

Recovering Lost Face

The post-totalitarian blues are haunting the countries of the other Europe.

—Rupnik (1995:61)

AFTER 1989

The political geography of Central and Eastern Europe changed when the power of long-term national regimes failed under the pressures of local insurgencies and economic collapse. In Czechoslovakia liberation from the totalitarian political regime followed the Velvet Revolution in 1989. A public demonstration on Black Friday, November 17, 1989, was led by students, workers and actors. "On November 17, however, the police were confronted by thousands of unknown, young faces who had started to come to terms with their fear" (Wheaton and Kavan 1992). During the following week demonstrations initiated the resignation of the Communist leadership (see Wheaton and Kavan 1992).

In the early 1990s, after political changes in Czechoslovakia, Soviet occupiers were forced to leave the cities and army bases. Rapid political change in Central and Eastern Europe shifted power and made possible the development of new political projects. This new political reality and the new dilemma of belonging to Europe has been discussed by Jacques Rupnik (Rupnik 1995). For Rupnik the contemporary desire of Czechs is to belong to a new Europe, a contemporary Europe rather than what he identified as another Europe, the former Communist Eastern Europe (Rupnik 1995). In his early work *The Power of the Powerless,* Václav Havel wrote, "A specter is haunting eastern Europe: the specter of what in the West is called 'dissent'" (Havel 1990). Post-totalitarian Eastern Europe is haunted by collective memories of the past.

Today, in the Czech Republic,[1] as well as in other post-socialist countries, the desire to reconcile is not limited to survivors of camps, prisoners, and dissidents. People from the youngest generation are interested in capturing Mukls' memories. Asking questions about crimes, punishment and forgiveness related to the Communist regimes in Central and Eastern Europe is not the domain of narrow academic and intellectual circles, but part of a wider public dialog. The individual and collective consciousness, a live organ of the human body, has joined a struggle for truth.

The second part of this book is about Mukls' collective and individual desires to recover their mutual relatedness and their future hopes, while coming to terms with their alienation from others—non-Mukls. I will discuss this process as a reconciliation. Mukls' modes of reconciliation include their counter rituals to state violence, their organized annual communal events. These are the extraordinary times during which large numbers of participating Mukls are together. I will also present other forms of togetherness, ordinary, day-to-day times. Mukls returning from their celebrations find themselves on the rim of society.

I present two types of evidence, showing significant parts of Mukls' lives today: their annual memorial gathering in Jáchymov, a former uranium mine and labor camp; and a hospital visit with Čeněk by a small group of Mukl friends in Prague. I will discuss various ways Mukls are relating, to each other and to others—non-Mukls—and inventing their new language of reconciliation. I ask, What kind of subject positions are available as places from which suffering may be voiced? What are the forms through which aging Mukls express their desire to heal? Two major aspects of Mukls' recovering seem to unite individual and collective efforts at reconciliation, relationship to time and the politics of voice and face. When examining the location of Mukls' voice and recovery of face, I often work through the analytical category of time. However, I do not think of time as a fixed or universal category, and I agree with Carol Greenhouse (Greenhouse 1996) that time is not a unified force, the property of a whole society, but rather that it "divides people within their societies" (Greenhouse 1996:76). In the context of my study, my aim is not to engage the meaning of time on a general, even a national level, but I simply point out different notions of time in relation to Mukls' reconciliation and memory of violence.

When confronted with the conditions of Muklhood today, I realized how important their annual memorial events are for Mukls. Since 1990, at the end of May and during much of June, these public celebrations have been held at former camps and prisons. I have attended meetings in camps at Příbram and Jáchymov; the prisons Bory in Plzeň and Pankrác in Prague; the national cemetery in Vyšehrad; the memorial to General Pika in Prague and a meeting in Šternberk Castle south of Prague. Every one of these memorial meetings is conducted annually on a fixed schedule. While I have visited one or another of these events every year since 1996, here I will present an analysis of the 2003 meeting in Jáchymov in which I participated. I also refer to Čeněk's return to Bory prison in Plzeň and to several autobiographical texts published by Mukls. I see that these events provide unique occasions for recovering lost face. Through examining Mukls' returns to the locations of their trauma, I recognize them as a language of reconciliation and acts of recovering Mukls' lost face.

While meeting with Mukls over a longer period of time, I learned significantly more about their collective politics, desires, and relatedness within their own community, which they identified as a family.[2] Because I am fascinated by their relationships both in the camps and after release, I dedicate a great deal of Part II of this book to this subject. I will further show how violence altered their sense of relating to others and how they reconfigured the notions of kinship and family. My discussion of kinship and family is far from the traditional anthropological understanding of kinship studies focused on descent theory, or residence rules and domestic organization. I am concerned with how Mukls utilize kinship ties, how they conceived of family while subjected to violence and how they even expanded the notion of family when transforming friendship to kinship. Given the Czech cultural-biological constructions and constraints of family, this transformation was somewhat unexpected. In order to make my discussion of Mukls' kinship and family accessible, I need to introduce the Czech cultural-biological understanding of kinship and family.

In contrast to the social role of kinship and family in non-European and non-western societies, the Czechs, like other Europeans regard kinship and family as a matter of birth and the facts of biology. Fixed in the biological sense, the term *nuclear family* also defines what is domestic. As anthropologists observed elsewhere, domestic space and time are not determined by gender roles, but rather are carved out of public and private roles by exclusionary politics. In earlier chapters I have discussed the distinction between the public and private spheres in Czechoslovak society and emphasized how political discourse entered the domestic sphere through violence and how domesticity became a symbol of a safe zone, the gift of comfort.

As result, I argue here that domestic space is intimate, personal, and strangers are not usually welcome. Friends enter the domestic space only under rules governing particular times. Some Czechs would invite their friends to their homes for an evening drink and coffee, but not for dinner. When visiting, a small group of guests, often just one couple, is restricted to the living room. The big party, or open house, is not common in Czech society. In contrast to the United States, children rarely bring their friends home for play and never for sleepovers. Meals are shared only with the nuclear family except for holidays, when only grandparents, but not other extended family, may be invited. To this day, the home is a private and familial space only. In this light, Mukls' familial relatedness, formed in camps and prisons, is unique and extends traditional notions of Czech kinship and family boundaries.

A PLACE OF HELL: JÁCHYMOV LABOR CAMPS

Jáchymov was the location of several labor camps located around uranium mines in Western Bohemia.[3] Uranium, a commodity highly valued by the Soviets, was shipped to the Soviet Union. Soviet experts supervised the mining,[4] and Czechs provided cheap Mukl labor. These camps were administered from a central location in Ostrov.[5]

I focused on the event in Jáchymov because I perceive this return and remembering as symbolic of other memorial celebrations. I chose this celebration because it is well attended, by both Mukls and Muklyně, and it is one of the longer running gatherings. I contend that Mukls' conduct in Jáchymov is a form of ritual to counter the state violent rituals established in 1948.

This part of my narrative is based on my direct observations, informal and casual conversations, that took place while I was at Jáchymov. In addition, I include references to written reflections by Mukls about Jáchymov and life in the camps.

Mukls' living conditions in Jáchymov were harsh, difficult, dangerous, and for some deadly. Mukls characterized their days in Jáchymov as slave labor in the mines. They suffered hunger, cold, sleep deprivation, and daily exposure to uranium radiation. Yet, on these return visits, they also remember jokes, moments they shared and glimpses of the beauty in the natural landscape surrounding the camps.

"Already by 1945 the Russian Army had occupied Jáchymov. It was one of the few areas in the world known at the time for uranium mines that were open for mining" (Hejl and Kaplan 1986). The Soviets held the Czechoslovak government responsible for finding mining labor to satisfy their demand for uranium. A desperate government found the solution, the labor camps. Pejskar wrote about this: "In the fall of 1948, right after the putsch, the Communist government began building concentration camps" (Pejskar 1987:204). The government's official name for these camps was *Tábory nucených prací* (TNP), forced labor camps.[6]

In her historical article on the Jáchymov camps, Petrašová in addition to providing a history of Jáchymov uranium mining also presented statistical data on the number[7] of political prisoners in Jáchymov between 1949 and 1958 (Babka and Veber 2002).[8] Jáchymov is one of the places to which Mukls return every year for their annual celebration of survival and for a memorial to the victims. Since the first meeting in 1990 the number of participants has declined.[9]

I call this section Jáchymov Hell, and its structure is based on three major activities organized every year during the Jáchymov meeting.[10] The Mukls' program in Jáchymov includes individual or small-group visits to actual camps and mines on Friday, a formal ceremony conducted on the Jáchymov square on Saturday morning, and a participants gathering in a local movie theater for a public discussion and forum on Saturday afternoon.

Having attended similar events at six other locations since 1996, I found that the Jáchymov meeting resembled each of the others in its general features. I am using the Jáchymov event in this book as an overall structural framework for the sections that follow. I will examine the Mukls' campground walk, the Saturday morning ceremonial gathering, and their afternoon forum. While there are different histories, different occasions for gathering, and, of course, different individuals at each location, the event at Jáchymov may be viewed as the common structural framework within which such notions as solidarity and fragmentation, darkness and hope, silence and voice, face and defacement, camaraderie and alienation, and justice and fictive political power regularly recur. These notions are embodied in many Mukls' counter-rituals, but also are part of their memory constituted in ordinary, everyday life.

The camp is the space that opens up when the state of exception starts to become the rule.

—Agamben (2000)

High up in the mountains, icy cold, with people being fired on every other moment, with people being killed. . . . Hundreds of men in tatters waiting to see what will happen to them next. And beyond the wire are black, hostile mountains.

—Mucha (1967)

It was a place where life was so unbearable that the Mukls call it Jáchymov Hell. Jáchymov is a place of double register on the map of the Czech lands. This small town stretching through a narrow mountain valley on the border between Germany and northwest Czech Republic is known for its spa, a place of healing. It is also remembered by Mukls as hell, a place of eighteen forced labor camps, uranium mines, and a place of intended liquidation.[11] For Mukls the camp is not a historical fact, belonging to the past, but it is "the hidden matrix and *nomos* of the political space in which we still live" (Agamben 2000:36).

When walking in the hills of Jáchymov during the summers of 2003 and 2004, Mukls and I visited the locations of their former camps. In the forest, small overgrown fields cover up the last remains of the housing facilities. As the Mukls and I walked to the places in the hills where the uranium mines were hidden and where concentration camp barracks once stood, here over invisibly radioactive earth, Mukls Jiří, Jarda and Luboš[12] reconstructed wintertime in the camp.

Jiří: The camp kitchen and laundry room was built on a concrete frame, but the barracks where we lived were built on wooden pilings. You could see underneath these buildings. The temperature never rose above zero. I remember someone spilled some coffee on the floor and it didn't melt until spring.

Jarda: Here was the gate, the entrance to the camp.

Luboš: And over there you can see the highest hill, Barbora, I was there forty months. It was a camp where the first snow came down in September and the last in June. The most beautiful view was from Barbora.

Jarda: But we could never see it all. From one window you could only see half of the mountain Cinovec. From other parts of the building others could see the other half. That was intentional architectural planning. (At this Mukls are laughing. . . .)

Jiří: Many camps are gone, they are overgrown today. Here was the cultural center. The most stupid of the guards were our tutors, because they couldn't do anything else. One day one of them said, "A dollar is not worth thirty-four crowns, but seven crowns. You will see, they will all crawl over our borders from the West."

Luboš: Once we had a lot fun. One of them said, "You think we don't know that you are talking about how stupid we are, and us but we do know . . . ha, ha, ha."

Jiří: We had a lot of fun. One of them said, "I can't wait until we march in front of the White House in New York." We couldn't stop laughing.

Luboš: One time I came back to recall the physical organization of the camp. So I closed my eyes and imagined it was there . . . and that was over there.

Jiří: . . . and over there was a camp where they concentrated the criminals.

Jarda: I remember it was called the killers valley.

Jiří: Today the camps are gone, and you see a lot of summer cottages. That is something! Radioactive gardens for recreation. Once we discovered that adding water to low content ore would give a higher uranium reading. So we had some fun with them. The Russians were crazy for uranium. They took uranium for gold.

Luboš: Two guys were running away, and they waited for them in the city and shot them down.

Jirka: Lets go to Nikolaj (camp name), to see where we lived.

Jarda: Everyday we marched eight hundred meters from camp to work.

Jirka: I remember the eclipse of the sun. We were marching in the Russian bus.

Luboš: We had to hold the waist of the Mukl ahead of us and march.

Jiří: We—five hundred men—marched here in the Russian bus (also called the Jáchymov bus). Marching in the bus meant that we had to form lines and stand together while bound by metal wire around our formation. It was worse when the metal wire was old and sharp. The front rows of men marched fast, but the last had to run to keep up with the group. Once there was an eclipse of the sun. We found lying around small pieces of glass, which we smoked over a fire until the glass was dark. While marching in the bus we were looking through the dark glass at the sun.

Luboš: One time, when we were staying in line, there were eighty of us. . . . Before we knew it there were 3,500 people in this camp. They closed the Jáchymov camps in 1958.

Jiří: They shipped us elsewhere.

Walking with Mukls over their old camps, there in the middle of a dense forest, gave me special insights into their ways of remembering. Their collective memory was not cohesive, but rather spontaneous and interactive. It was a play, a re-enactment of their past deeply connected to their present. Their intrinsic memory of time in the camps, as it was performed in front of me, was fragmented and, yet, rich with multiple themes and experiences. It was the most unmediated reconciliation I have experienced with Mukls. What struck me as most intriguing about this counterritual to pain and suffering was the presence of a linguistic code switch. When speaking, they moved between the notions of beauty and coarseness, from death to laughter. It was through the contrast in their voices, the multiple registers, that I became familiar with Mukls' time.

There is a different duality from the novelist Karel Pecka.[13] In his *Motáky Nezvěstnému* (1980) he wrote about the Mukls' bus. When asked later, in an interview by the historian Bartošek, about the authenticity of the bus, Pecka confirmed it, and added:

The view from outside is effective, artistically even poetic, but think about the possibility of being inside this bus, and literature can do that, investigate the

"bus" from inside . . . it is a tragedy to lose speed while marching, the metal wire
can cut you in half, in front they scream one-two, one-two, around are dogs and
guys with guns, that is the picture. (Bartošek 2001:37)

The multiple experiences the novelist Pecka wrote about also occur in the
memories of other Mukls. For many Mukls, a return to the camps triggered a reconstruction of time, which often seemed bimodal, at once tragically comforting
and intensely painful. I discussed Mukls' sense of time in the context of arrest
and identified their structural time as durational. In this chapter I will discuss two
other dimensions of Mukls' sense of time, cyclical and historical time.[14]

During one of my fieldwork visits in Prague, I stayed at my friend's
house. It was a three-generation household and because of their generosity,
I became part of the family. They shared meals and conversations with me,
and were very interested in my research topic. When I returned from Mukls'
meetings, I would often share my observations from Mukls' gatherings with
my host family. One afternoon, in the company of my friend's mother, the
grandmother of the family, I talked about these annual returns in relation
to Mukls' sense of cyclical time. She raised her head from her ironing and
said, "For me it is the month of May. I feel sick every year. May was when
I returned from the Nazi concentration camp. I was just a little girl, when
my father died in the camp after liberation and I walked out by myself
and then went all the way to Prague. My whole life, every year in May,
I feel strange." That night, when my friend came home from work, I told
her about my conversation with her mother. Her face turned white and she
slowly replied, "You see, I was born in May." This subject of her mother's
suffering had never entered our conversation before, and in the silence that
followed, I sensed the restlessness, hidden deep inside her, because of being
forced to share her mother's pain. It was as if this trauma settled between
them and grew within their relationship. I realized then the brutal continuity
of violence as it had worked itself into the daughter's life and had become
part of her cyclical time. This episode made me more sensitive to notions
of time, and time has become an important analytical category in my own
research.

For the Mukl, time is measured in a sequence of traumatic events: arrest,
interrogations, and trial, but time is also cyclical in reference to participation
in annual memorial meetings. Anthropologists agree that the human attempt
to measure or remember time is closely bound to culture. Challenging the
idea of a single and objective sense of time or space, he emphasized a strong
relationship between space and time in social life as well as material links
between politico-economic and cultural processes. In his view, cyclical and
repetitive motion provides a sense of security in a personal world. When our

world is ruptured by depression, recession, war or social disruption, we often reassure ourselves with the idea of cyclical time as a natural phenomenon to which we must adapt as "the perpetual counterpoint to progress" (Harvey 1990:202). Harvey's perception of time and space is important to my conceptualization of Mukls' reconciliation. When they return to former camps, structural location intersects with the cyclical and historical value of their time. I will argue along with Langer (1991) that remembering their closeness to death in the camps (here Langer is investigating Holocaust survivors' memories) creates a separation and alienation that can never be overcome. As Langer puts it: "The survival of trauma is not to heal, but endure and the previous experience can't be undone by the next" (Langer 1991:56). Langer's argument is that memory is not neutral, and remembering trauma is durational as well as chronological. What may be chronological narratives to an audience can be for a mental witness; that is, the narrator remembering "out of time" (Langer 1991:55), durational time. Durational time resists and undermines, invades chronology according to Langer, which leaves an authors' memory and time in dialog: "The one celebration of life that has just ended in the sadness of death, transcendent by a 'normal' future for those who remain; the other signifying a death that has not been preceded by a life connected to such an end followed by a temporal void" (Langer 1997).

Jáchymov Hell is a place where Mukls gather every year during the last weekend in May. Mukls return to the old and familiar places marked by their own pain. The Mukls' ceremonial return to the camps began in 1990. Male political prisoners, who lived through Jáchymov Hell, now return every year to reconcile in this place. The Mukls' annual memorial weekend is a time of remembering, reuniting, and reconciling. Mukls also organize returns to other work camps—Příbram (I attended in 1996), or prisons like Bory (I attended in 2001), Pankrác (I attended in 2003), Pardubice, and Leopoldov. I see these returns as symbolic of Mukls' recovering of their face, the face once hidden behind the walls of camps and prisons.

Jáchymov narratives are part of the "survivor's struggle to find a means of reestablishing authorship over their stories" and at the same time a place of "collective authorization of individual experience" (Das 1997:12). Mukls' narratives, as told in Jáchymov during their walks in the hills, are a part of the language of reconciliation. In Jáchymov they share narratives of the individual and collective experiences. By retelling the story, Mukls are "creating a different kind of past" for themselves, one that is based on their dealing "with the violence of memories in the present" (Das and Kleinman 1997:13).

Returns are also one of the opportunities for Mukls to share their narratives with one another. The memorial events are also their opportunity to express publicly their remembering, reconnecting, solidarity, and friendship. Mukls' conversations about their own experiences in the Communist concentration camps and life afterwards in Czechoslovakia contain rich, multilayered testimony about the conditions of the political other both under the Communist, Stalinist, political order and after its fall. Mukls' stories are not just verbal glimpses of the past, but are narratives of pain reflecting the Mukls' everydayness both now and in the past.

Jiří Sochor described his experience in Jáchymov:

> My first impression of the camp was devastating. They lined us up in groups of five, they were screaming at us, pushing us from all sides, and running around us like mad dogs. The first night we spent in the "cultural hall" sleeping on the floor. It was a big room elevated off the ground. The next day after such a night I couldn't walk straight. After that I was sent to Camp Eliaš. If it weren't for this terrible reality, it would have been a lovely part of the world; the camp was located on the top of the mountain and surrounded by forests from both sides, and above was a different camp, "Rovnost". (. . .) In the night the whole space was under intense light from reflectors, shining like a city. Across the space were wires everywhere. Shortly after I arrived to this hell, they established another Camp Eliaš II. (Pejskar 1987:210)

Jáchymov camps and mines, just as prisons, camps and mines in other locations in Czechoslovakia, were known by name to Mukls, and they were familiar with the different conditions among these institutions. Among the Mukls, Camp Eliaš was famous.

> Camp Eliaš I. which became my "home" was situated by the leaders' house. In front was a big place where we had to gather three times a day to be counted. This service was done by guards who didn't belong to the camp, from the gate they were led by an elder of the camp, who was most often drunk. . . . Prisoners lived in six big wooden barracks, built in a circle. Part of the barracks was old with wooden bunk beds covered with roaches. Prisoners had to take the beds out sometimes to clean off the roaches. Roaches were cramped together in huge bunches, it was a disgusting picture. At the corners of the camps were located towers with armed guards. . . . Later Camp Eliaš was moved to the location of camp Vykmanov. It was an old army camp, probably built during the Austro-Hungarian empire. . . . In this camp prisoners suffered from terrible hunger.
>
> It was worst in the winter, if you didn't fall sleep by nine o'clock you would shiver all night. Often it was unbearable. Prisoners dreamed about food. We dreamed about bread and black coffee. Prisoners were falling down during the morning gatherings on the "apelplatz." I saw them fighting over food in the trash by the kitchen. Not everybody. Some maintained their pride, even in such conditions. Others collapsed in spite of their intelligence and education. The guards saw the ones who kept their pride as dangerous. . . . Soviets took care of the machinery in the Jáchymov mines. These machines didn't function when they arrived. Also, other materials and equipment were not very good. The mines

were built poorly and many people died in them. They were not well drained, they were wet and unhealthy, smelling of decaying trash, septic waste and debris from explosions. (Pejskar 1987: 213)

In the introduction to the novel *Motáky Nezvěstnému* (Pecka 1980), Václav Černý characterized Jáchymov work camps.

The transport to Jáchymov, in Krušné Hory (a small mountain range) one lágr after the other, everyone is there for years: lágr "Braterstvi" (Brotherhood), in mines Svornost, lágr of plague "Nikolaj," for three years of hunger; who didn't go through it has no full experience of humanity, is an incomplete person, because human life there is reduced to the gift of air, sleep, warmth, bread and water; the camp of punishment "Elko," lágrs mortuary of black death from inhaling microscopic dust from the mined uranium, with the highest concentration of gamma light (radiance), in the space directed/controlled by the Soviet experts—of what? Engineering or counterespionage? (Pecka 1980:11)

Mukl Václav Vaško describes in his memoir his arrival at the center of the Czechoslovak Gulag.

I received a new number: AO-22400. Camp Nikolaj, where I was brought, was spread out on the hills of Krušné Hory. The beauty and peaceful nature was disturbed by the wooden barracks of the camp, which was surrounded by a high fence of twisted wire. On each of the four corners was a guard tower with a machine gun nest. This conjured up the image of a Nazi concentration camp. In front of me was the rectangular square with the *apelplatz* (roll call place), around the barracks. Next to the gate was the commandant's barrack, in the middle a cultural barrack and hospital, opposite was the kitchen, dining room, showers with a drying room for work clothes, all the way to the left was the "correction" (solitary confinement) with a bed sheet instead of glass in the window, at the far end was a toilet. (Vaško 1999:194)

My first impression? The good one: space, mountains, forests, planes, and clear, wonderful, slightly sharp mountain air. The terrible: The afternoon shift ready for departure. The black mass of Mukls, dressed from head to heels in rubber. A number of coughing lines. Even to this day I can hear those dry coughs. "Don't be troubled, that is the Jáchymov laugh;[15] soon you will have it as well."

My first shift. Alarm at four, breakfast, lineup. I always line up in the back. Mistake! Unexpectedly the elder of the shift came up to me, gives me the pole with the metal wire on it and said to wrap wire around the lined up Mukls. As if hypnotized I listened, I unwound the wire binding them waist high, and at the same time I am conscious of tying up my friends. I told the elder with resolution that next time I will not lower myself with such cruelty. (Vaško 1999:196)

Vaško's testimony reflects the remembering of details from Mukls' life in one of the camps. Just as Vaško drew an analogy between Communist camps and Nazi camps, some other prisoners would refer in their narratives to Nazi camps. Jaromír, one of the Mukls I met at Ganys and interviewed in 1995, remembered his arrival.

> The camp was surrounded with two lines of sharp wire. Every one hundred meters were located towers with strong lights. By the entrance were a large number of guards with dogs. Above the main gate was a sign, just as in Nazi camps, *Arbeit macht frei* (Work Is Freedom). After I entered the camp I became just a number—068.

For Mukls, Nazi camps were the ultimate measure for the level of cruelty. They became a number or as many said a commodity. A Mukl is a *hmota obalená hadry a poháněná buzerac* (a substance wrapped in rags and powered by harrassment) wrote Lubomír Školoud and Petr Štěpánek in their book about Muklhood (Školoud and Štěpánek 1992). Mukls' memories of camps are consistent with Arendt's perspectives that concentration and liquidation camps are laboratories for the regime to test the endless possibilities of political power and the goal of concentration camps is to transform humans into commodities. In Mukls' memories, once again, there is a passage framed in relationship to the formation of subject. It involves facing death, but in this case the transformation of subject in the camp expands over a long period of time. In contrast to the early rites of arrest, interrogation and trial, violent rituals filled the ordinary, day-to-day life.

With the work of time, "the space of death" (Feldman 2001:86 and Taussig 1987:469) became Mukls' ordinary condition. That life was what Giorgio Agamben defines as "bare life," *zoe* in contrast to *bios* (Agamben 2000). Bare life is not natural life, but the result of political power; through fundamental acts of sovereignty, it is the sense of being included in the political realm by virtue of being excluded. From the time I first met the small group at Café Ganys, I wondered how they, Mukls, coped with all that they had endured.

Agamben, in his philosophy of political life, pointed out that concentration camps are the expression of the great totalitarian states' power in the twentieth century. He defined such spaces: "The people who entered the camp moved about in a zone of indistinction between the outside and the inside" (Agamben 2000). Agamben raised an interesting set of points with regard to the logic and rationale for the camps. He wrote, "It is only because the camps constitute a space of exception—a space in which the law is completely suspended—that everything is truly possible in them" (Agamben 2000:39). Camp, as a political space absent every juridical protection, is a final solution, and as Agamben put it, "Inasmuch as its inhabitants have been stripped of every political status and reduced completely to naked life, the camp is also the most absolute biopolitical space that has ever been realized—a space in which power confronts nothing other than pure biological life without any mediation" (Agamben 2000:40).

Agamben's concern with the nature of the camp is focused on the notions of time and space in the context of state violence. He sees the birth of camps as arising from the relationship between order and the modern nation-state's territory. On the one hand this is boundried territory, a space in which one's life is reduced to naked or bare life. Yet in the context of the state's imposition of total political power, indistinction of the boundries dividing in and out negate the very nature of the camp. The structure of the camp is created regardless of the nature of the crimes committed. The camp is, for Agamben, the product of state exceptions.

The Communist camps had a certain ambiguity about them when compared to Nazi concentration camps. Prisoners struggled for a long time, ten to fifteen years, to understand what was going on. Many Mukls expressed that part of their every day was their thinking about the collapse of totality (totalitarian political power). Nothing was clear and everything was ambiguous for many Mukls, but the possibility of the end of their imprisonment was on their minds everyday. Mukl Jiří remembered: "We thought it will crack any minute, we believed that western countries will get involved and help us be liberated from Sovietization and the inhuman treatments we were subjected to." Jiří's expressed the expectation of outside Western help, is a very important political-psychological moment. Its relevence lies within Mukls' political sense of connectedness,[16] of reaching beyond national borders. This political consciousness was, based on what Jiří and other Mukls said during our talks, an important psychological moment of hope for the future. This sense of belonging to a larger, global community opened the possibility for Mukls to see totalitarian political power in the light of their temporality.

Temporality and violence, as pointed out by Poole (Poole 1994), are significant notions when victims make sense of their positions. For some Mukls, consciousness of temporality while being interrogated, tortured and imprisoned in the camps made it possible to withstand the violence. The temporality became one of their means of survival. The loss of moral ethics, within the practices of violent rituals, became, for Mukls, an important sign of the fragility of political power and allowed them to hope for its eventual fall. Poole, when discussing the specifics of culturally and historically bounded acts of violence, wrote, "By recognizing that violence is politically contingent and dependent on the moment in which it occurs, they come instead to perceive that power is itself inherently contestable and unstable" (Poole 1994:272).

I read in Jiří's and other testimonies that Mukls' understanding of this violence was, from its beginnings, based on their recognition of temporality in political power. The absence of ethics in totalitarian political power, in the Mukls' case, led to their understanding of its temporality. Long-term imprisonment worked against the power of temporality, but Mukls' believed, as they remember it, that their exclusion from the public space and their defacement was temporal, as was totalitarian political power.

> *A year has elapsed underground, and what happened during this time will now begin to repeat itself—work, the pit, the eternal darkness below ground, while up above summer will draw to a close, autumn will come and with it the silent blue mists in the valley.*

> —Mucha (1967:22)

CONFIGURATIONS OF KINSHIP AND FAMILY

> *Yesterday was Sunday—Visiting Day. . . . When I see the men's families waiting outside in the road, in the heat and dust, after a long journey for the sake of a short half hour, my heart aches at the thought that I have to bring such suffering on these whose lives I would like to make easier.*

> —Mucha (1967:20)

When Mukls returned from the camps they faced not only a society different from the era prior to their arrest but also changes in their relationships with families and friends. I discussed various forms of ruptures of kinship ties under the newly empowered totalitarian political system in Czechoslovakia. Denial of contact with family from the time of arrest, denial of information about the arrested individuals, verbal and psychological blackmail, as well as threats against family members during interrogations became major means of punishment inflicted by the state. The project of total exclusion and forced isolation of the enemy became the central focus of the state-sanctioned violence.[17] Well-organized state control of contact between prisoners and families is evident in Mukls' testimonies, in published biographies,[18] and systematically documented by historians Hejl and Kaplan (1986). The denial of contact with a spouse became an effective psychological torture that continued after the trial and throughout the time served in the camps. Hilda spoke about the disconnection from her family.

> First we were allowed to write only eight lines, then later sixteen. They moved me from place to place and didn't bother to send my mail. For a year I didn't know about my family. My father died when I was in prison, but I didn't know for a long time. My son was sixteen years old and a very good student. When I was in prison he was sent to a forced labor camp to serve his army duty, where he became ill with jaundice. My mother sent me a card about his transport to the hospital, but then I didn't know about him for a year. I didn't know if he is

alive or not. Pain was eased by our mutual comfort, thanks to our good group. Camaraderie was always there. We trusted each other and always kept contact. That was the worst for women. They knew where we were most vulnerable. One time they put a pistol to my head and said: You have a son, and now you don't, we can take care of it. When I was in the prison Litomerice, they put us for a while in Terezin fortress (former Nazi death camp). For visits with family we were temporarily transported back to Litomerice. I could see only one person, and say nothing about my life or where we were. Armed guards supervised visits.

Mukl Rudolf remembers family visits, "My wife brought my son. He was still very young. They let him sit on my lap. He was silent, just sat on my lap without words. That took five minutes and then they had to go."

Short visits, sporadically allowed, were from the Mukls' perspective, a painful re-connecting rather than a time for maintaining bonds. The number of visitors was limited to two per Mukl. When I asked Mukls more about the visits, they remember them as short and silent moments of togetherness. Čeněk explained, "A visit was permitted only once every three months for ten minutes. It was hard, like being ripped from the prison environment and once again a reminder of the past life. My wife came with her mother. She was strong; she waited for me eleven years." Loss of family life was deeply felt by the Mukls. In their narratives they expressed much deeper pain over relational loses than over any other ruptures of their lives before arrest. Mucha, in his journal from the camps, compared the visits of relatives to visiting a cemetery.

We are talked about in the past tense and even though reason argues that we exist, emotionally we have ceased to belong to the living. And thus visiting day is like a visit to family graves—a few tears, and a few memories, and a bunch of fresh dahlias. For many it means upheaval of a dearly bought tranquility. That I think, is the saddest thing about being a prisoner; in order to survive one has to kill in oneself all that one has loved. (Mucha 1967:20)

The denial of kinship and family, the punishment from the state, led to alienation, to social invisibility, and eventually to a form of social death. "We lived, we worked, but we did not exist. . . . Our being is a fact for ourselves; for everybody else we are somewhere between life and death" (Mucha 1967:20). Alienation was one of the major consequences for political others. Yet through such punishment prisoners gained a new belonging, belonging to the community of fellow political prisoners. Jiří D. spoke to me about their mutual connectedness: "This need to connect with former political prisoners is because we are practically one family. It is an irony, it is an absurdity, but we were the only free group in this country. We could do and say what we liked." How can we understand the meaning of the freedom that Jiří talks about? How can we begin to understand when Jiří says, "We could do and say what we liked," when we know that these prisoners were in forced labor camps? The prison, the guards, and the prison regime controlled their lives, and yet Jiří remembers the experience of freedom within the prison. Jiří's narratives take us back to Čeněk's return to his former prison. After years it was as if he were returning to his home. But as Jiří's voice suggests, his comfort was not only from being in the familiar space of prison, but also in new Mukls' relatedness. A Mukl often refers to the Mukl community as family. The meaning of these new family relationships between prisoners, both male and female, during their time in camp became the foundation for their own place of freedom as they struggled together to survive. Through shared punishment the prisoners gained a new belonging—a political prisoners' family belonging. The violent rituals, horrendous working conditions, poor health and, most important, the shared experience of the denial of the old belonging led to their new configuration of kinship.

Political prisoners' shared communal experience in prison created a deeply embedded solidarity. This solidarity, an essential means of survival, served also as a basis for a mechanism of alienation from friends, family and the rest of society outside the prison. (See the testimony from a Mukl's wife in the section on interrogations). One of the Muklyně spoke about such solidarity.

> We protected ourselves as best we could against organized violence, or we may call it genocide. Only a small group of people can imagine how special it was to be with people of the same interests. The escapes to the world of literature, poetry, music and art. That was our water of life, helping us to survive. In the camps under harsh slave labor, we developed a unique brotherhood. There were persons who failed and betrayed, but there were also personalities who held together the others. (Babka and Veber 2002)

The prisoners' consciousness of outside and inside worlds often led to alienation from the outside world and conversely to mutual solidarity inside the prison. Mukls' contact with the outside world was only through short visits from relatives occurring after long intervals, and as Čeněk revealed, the visit was a painful reminder of life outside the prison. The conscious polarity of outside and inside was a painful realization for many. Some Mukls also asked: "What kind of world is this in which so many people find the misery of prison more bearable than a return to the arms of society" (Mucha 1967:211)? In a previous discussion, I showed how, in Mukls' consciousness, the polarity between outside and inside is connected to their concept of prison becoming home. Consciousness of outside and inside is also, as discussed above, connected to belonging. They, Mukls, articulate that belonging as membership in the Mukls' family.

DURATIONAL TIME AND DIALOGIC SPEECH

In June 2001 I was invited to a conference held by the Czech-American Society for Art and Science in the city of Plzeň. One of the panels focused on Communist repression in 1948. Among the invited speakers was Mukl Čeněk, who had been imprisoned at Bory. Since Bory, one of the infamous Communist prisons, was located in Plzeň, for Čeněk this was a place of return. He spoke at the conference about his experience.

> Plzeň, the city in West Czech, became a symbolic place for me. In Plzeň the history of the twentieth century played out. My heart is pulling me to the familiar places in Bory prison like to a home. In 1949 Heliodor Pika, a distinguished Czech Army general was executed; Jan Šmíd, the doctor, was there and he gave Pika's family Pika's last cigarette butt.
>
> The beatings were a daily routine on *corrections* especially among the hard solitude cells. The "flying six" (an infamous group of guards) made us walk in a circle as if we were ducks, and then the ones who just fell down were carried to their cells. During the interrogations they threatened you with the death penalty for your whole family. They were forcing my wife to divorce me and my father had to move out to Slovakia.
>
> In Pankrác (Prague prison) was the cell of death. The executions did not occur until fourteen months after the trial. During the Nazi regime whoever was not executed after ninety days was given amnesty from the death penalty (this cannot be historically verified). The ones who were in Nazi prisons had to accomplish fifteen dkg of feather work (cleaning feathers) per day, we had to do sixty–seventy-five dkg per day. (Plzeň Bory 2002)

Considering Čeněk's return as symbolic of other returns, I will draw from his speech to show the dialogic character of Mukls' language of reconciliation. I will present multiple voices in their communication as they try to recover their lost public face.

Čeněk's conference speech included multiple voices, the voice of facing death, in contrast to the voice of prison as home. Double remembering of prison, a linguistic moment of "double register" (Bakhtin 1996), opens the possibility for reading multiple levels of intertextual meanings. The prisoners' language here has the character of a dialogue, identified by linguist Bakhtin as "heteroglossic" (Bakhtin 1996); that is, a multiplicity of voices in a language discourse. Čeněk was touched emotionally by returning and yet, in our conversation, he described Bory prison as one the worst of its time.

> I think a distinct characteristic for Bory prison was its medieval style. I saw prisoners walking inside metal cages in a circle. They were brought back from work camps to be punished. It went on for years without washing, showering

and a haircut. I could see their feet swollen from metal chains and their teeth were missing from the beatings. It was also in Bory prison where guards went to the pub and came back drunk and beat prisoners.

The concept of the prison becoming home emerged in others' testimonies. In his interviews with political prisoners, historian Karel Bartošek (Bartošek 2001) asked Mukl Pecka about his state of mind in terms of return from the camps. Pecka replied: "Puzzled. What will happen, how would I manage, what can I do? Because in the camp one had a sense of security" (Bartošek 2001:32). Bartošek asked a further question, "Did the *lágr* become home?" (Bartošek 2001:33) and Pecka responded: "There was the sense of security. You know that there, if they send you somewhere, you know what you can find and that nothing can happen to you, and that is how I would describe the feeling. But outside it was a different world. The way life is you knew only from a distance, from hearing about it" (Bartošek 2001:33).

From Pecka's narratives it is evident that the camp, for some Mukls, became over time a place of comfort in contrast to the outside world. The outside world, as Pecka indicated, had over time become unknown and imaginary. A place of darkness and bare survival, the prison, ironically, offered a sense of secure and even comforting being. "Wooden beds in the *lágr* never cooled off, because as soon as one shift left, the previous one is in it. I am now laying on one and suddenly the idea came to me this is perhaps the environment of my real home, since in the home of our fathers it is impossible to live. One's own home became as impossible to reach as a horizon beyond the twisted wire" (Pecka 1980:226).

The prisoners, caught in the misery of the camp, a place of hell, found themselves in paradoxically twisted conditions. The workings of time turned the prison experience into an expression of comfort, of familiarity. For some, the memories of the camp became memories of a home. This strange nextness, the prison as hell and home, has developed over time. The hegemonic power, as it was embodied in Mukls' belonging to camps, became synonymous with their agency for survival.

Mukls expressed insecure feelings when released in the early or mid-1960s. Society had changed since the time when they were arrested. This indicates that Mukls' notion of camp and its predictability as a home stood in contrast to their sense of alienation from life outside of prison. Mukls learned to survive in the camps. Facing death was part of their everyday. Their concept of prison as a home, as paradoxical as it may be, is helpful to understanding the duality of their situation. Today, as they refer to camp, it is in a peculiar way, as the space of death and also as their home.

Taking into consideration the dialogic character of language allowed me to examine the multiple register within Mukls' conversations during annual events such Jáchymov. I noticed that their conversations were charged with joking. As Mukls' dark stories entered deeper to my own life, I found comfort in their sense of humor. Their "joking relations" brought light to our memorial return trips. Humor made itself felt in several forms: in short remembered episodes, in performances directly described as a joke, or in the general sense of humor that was palpable during all the Mukls' social gatherings. Now, I have come to think of Mukls' humor as a language pattern particular to their community, their "languaculture" (Agar 1994).[19]

> **Franta:** I remember once I called Jiří. Jiří came with his friend leaning on his shoulder dressed in my nightgown with medals on the chest made from a tin can. They pretended to be soldiers from the Soviet Army. The camp's leaders gave them a week of hard "prison," but the best joke was the announcement from the camp loudspeaker that said: "For insulting the Soviet Army."
> When Jirka was dying of cancer I took him twice to the hospital and on the way his eyes looked sad, but he tried to joke until the end.

The ability to make a joke meant turning the language of pain into a different form of communication. Humor—inseparable from the Mukls' "language frame" (Agar 1994) is built into their grammar. Humor is the significant transmitter and a strategy for conveying the message. Humor is another register of Mukls' social togetherness, cohesion and solidarity. Joking has become the labor of making remembering pleasant. Communal joking in this instance is shared "language craft" (Agar 1994) developed as a strategy for the maintenance of distance from the trauma embodied in the consciousness of liquidation. Humor, as a form of language, is inextricably linked to the conditions of Muklhood.

When spending time with the Mukls I have noticed that a sudden wave of humor can overpower the shared memory of hell and make the next conversation possible. Mukls Franta and Jiří had real difficulty with speaking about their own pain or even remembering the pain of others, but they talked openly about joking in the camps. One of the Mukls reflected, "It is interesting that from Jáchymov Hell, what stays in the memory are funny stories and these stay in our heads more than the cruelties" (Babka and Veber 2002).

Expanded notions of Mukls' relatedness sprang from configuration of their kinship, a redefined sense of family, their alternative location of home, and the comfort they found in their newly developed language. In this sense the state's terror was counter-productive and as Pecka put it,

"We live! Unfortunately castrated, with a broken spine and an injured soul, but we are alive!" (Pecka 1980).

FRAGMENTATION: RUMORS AND LEGACY OF THE ARCHIVE

The division between inside (camp) and outside does not mean that the community inside was homogeneous. As a result of their personal occupational, religious, and age differences, diversity among Mukls was a given from the beginning. Yet these external sources contributing to the work camps' diversity were not as lasting or as destructive to Mukls' community as were newly developed forms of internal aspects of differences among Mukls. By internal aspects I mean, for example, rumors circulating in the camps, the regime's continuous interrogations, and the establishment of a leadership hierarchy in the work camps. These internal aspects of power structures caused continuous fragmentation of the Mukls' community. Mukls do not speak easily about internal fragmentation in the camps. Mukl Roman spoke about external and internal sources of divisions.

> In the *lágr* (camp) one gets to know people the way they are when they are naked. Life there was more intensive. The soul and mind were in training. There were people intellectually very strong next to simple ones, and the influence was great. One learned from the other.
>
> The people varied in professions and age. There were workers, farmers, students, priests, intellectuals, but also non-Mukls such as criminals, Nazis and their collaborators.

Many Mukls spoke of diversity the way Roman did, but in other narratives internal and external elements of difference are scattered throughout the text. Mukls testified that in the early years of their imprisonment the leaders were Nazi prisoners from World War II, referred to by the Mukls as *retribuční*.[20] They were in charge of different units in the camp and, according to Mukls, they were also in charge of other prisoners and often enjoyed privileges denied to ordinary prisoners. In Mukl Václav Paleček's narratives, published by Pejskar (1987), Paleček remembers,

> These people were used by the camp masters for acts of humiliation committed as state prisoners. The Mukl prisoners were sent to do hard labor, while these former Nazis were our commanders. In one of the camps I slept on the bed next to a prominent Nazi, Dr. Adler, his name we had placed during the WWII in London on a list of war criminals. (Pejskar 1987)

According to Mukls' narratives, when *retribuční* left the camps in 1952, Mukls were appointed to their positions. This hierarchy caused internal fragmentation among the Mukls. The hierarchical structure imposed on the Mukl family by the regime's advocates forced some Mukls to act as mediators between prisoners and guards. Being a mediator was cause for suspicion among the prisoners and was seen as an act of betrayal, which led to alienation between the Mukl mediators and other prisoners. It was only through the narratives of a few Mukls who were deeply affected by these internal forms of fragmentation that I learned about others' silence on this subject. Many emphasized how occupational diversity contributed to their mutual learning, but in contrast internal fragmentation was surrounded by silence.

One of the few Mukls who spoke about fragmentation was Vojta. I met Vojta in the office of the Confederation of Political Prisoners. He was very enthusiastic about helping other Mukls and active in the organization. In his interview, Vojta talked about his life and the terrible mistake that haunted him in the camp. He viewed his life as "a personal tragedy within a national tragedy."

My brother worked against the west, and our right wing politics, as a spy. He was caught by the CIC in West Germany and got twenty years in jail. Based on that, I made a decision to work against my brother's failures. I became a member of an antigovernment group. Our group was eventually discovered and the members arrested. It was spread as a rumor about me that I worked in the underground for my brother, who then was already arrested, and so it was the beginning of my big unhappiness, a camp within the camp. Fellow prisoners believed that I started an antigovernment group and then betrayed the whole group. The truth is I was innocent and couldn't prove it until 1968. Only then it was proven. Even my friend, who was also arrested, thought I was collaborating with my brother.

Later when I read my friend Franta my latest ethnographic text about Mukls, he began to talk about his position in the camp and his relationship to Vojta.

In the camp I was a *taborák* (a Mukl appointed to lead) and people came to me with rumors about somebody being left (politically left). I would say: "Do you have something specific?" Often they (camp police) spread rumors to divide us. Even when somebody was transferred the rumors came in or went out with him and so they circulated. Vojta's case is an example how one could get hurt by the spread of such rumors. He had a brother who worked for the Czech/Soviet police in Germany (he was in espionage for the KGB). In the camps, the Mukls often mistook Vojta for his brother. Mukls thought he was with "them" (police). Today Vojta and I are friends. He never said anything, but he knows I was on his side then.

Rumors in camps affected Mukls' relationships in poisonous ways. In many camps interrogations were part of ordinary camp life. Every call to interrogation in the camp brought both the experience of physical and psychological torture and suspicion on the part of the Mukl community directed against each prisoner called. At stake was the betrayal of others. While the possibility of a new, symbolic family gave Mukls a sense of belonging, interrogations provoked rumors of betrayal from within the Mukl family, which had been formed in the presence of continuous attempts by the state to fragment it. A rumor of betrayal among Mukls, then, became part of the state's power over the prisoners. The ability of rumor as a transmitter of power within a community has been considered by a number of scholars, but in particular Ranajit Guha (1999), who examined rumor in the context of the peasant insurgency in India.[21] Circulating rumors, as Guha relates was done in India, was an effective, unofficial transmitter for establishing communal mobility during the insurgency.

Rumors in the Czechoslovak labor camps were linked to the political fiction of the state. Rumor impacted on Mukls' relatedness, alienated many Mukls from their community while in prison, and continues to have an impact among Mukls today. Political fiction manifests itself in the most severe way when determining membership in the Confederation of Political Prisoners. Not all Mukls belong automatically. They must first verify their record in the state police archives. Within the Mukls' community political purity as a condition for membership in the Confederation is tied to the problem inherent in the notion of historical truth.[22] The rumor, like the archive, in the light of imagined political purity, has become the barrier blocking the pursuit of reconciliation for some.

Through Vojta and Franta's stories we can begin to unpack some of the elements of Mukls' reconciliation. Vojta was rehabilitated (the official term for "cleared") after many years, but Franta remained excluded till the end of his life. While he is connected to others, through Mukls' kinship, he cannot belong to the official organization, the Confederation of Political Prisoners. Listening to Franta's story, I realized I was in a peculiar position. Franta knew while telling me this that I had met with Mukls who told a different story regarding his role in the camp. It was as though he had to tell me his side of it in order to continue our friendship. I have already made the conceptual connection between Mukls' experience and the fictive character of the power structures. By then, I knew from his fellow Mukls, some from the group I met at Ganys, and others from the Confederation, how Franta had acted when he was in a position to help others in the camp. They told me about his acts of camaraderie and support. Yet the Confederation of Political Prisoners would not accept him because of the notations in his file.

This subject came up again when I interviewed Franta's son Petr. The son was angry, as if he too had been betrayed by his Mukl family. Growing up, he identified himself with the Mukls' family. When he was little he called his parents' friends, other Mukls, uncles and aunts. For Petr, Mukls were his family. Now, when his father was excluded from the Confederation, he was angry. His family had turned on him and his father after all. His identity was based on being a child of a Mukl and a Muklyně (his mother, Franta's wife, was also a prisoner); now after many years and after the end of political totality, he also experienced alienation. While his alienation was indirect, the process underscores the continuity of the Communist regime's fictive political power.

My first opportunity to discuss the rehabilitation (clearing) process directly with Mukls was in 1997, when I met two of the members of a reconciliation committee, Jitka and Rudolf. They were Mukls charged with administering the rehabilitation of individual Mukls in the Confederation of Political Prisoners (an organization established in 1990). Jitka, one of the Muklyněs from the board of the Mukls' organization said,

I was the judge on the (political prisoners' party) committee. The records are problematic, because people were categorized as an A, B, or C type of informant. A and B meant clearly collaboration, but category C didn't. People came from long distances, and (were) old, with the hope for rehabilitation, and it was not possible. We (judges) were restrained by rules for reconciliation. We had the case, for example, of an eighty-two-year-old man who had a record of being frequently interrogated at the police station. He claims that he had the agreement with his (insurgency) group, that he will go but will not tell anything. Yes, but today the members of his group are dead and no one can bear witness. In the prison it was different. When we stayed in one place a long time, we knew who was going to the "tower" too often, but the guards were careful as well. It is difficult.

Evidence of collaboration by Mukls, surrounded by secrecy, rumors, and ambiguity, is a painful subject for them. Some may disagree about who was an informant or agent, some wish not to talk about it at all, but most would agree that forcing them to collaborate was one of the methods the regime used against them. Fragmentation of the community is seen by some Mukls as one of the regime's greatest crimes because of its continuity. Rudolf, who was also an active member of the reconciliation committee, emphasized how such power exercised upon the Mukls was a constant cause of suffering. Knowing that he was familiar with individual archival files produced by the state secret police, I asked him to comment on the evaluations of these files.

Yes, some people were broken by the regime. After some people returned from prison, they tried to protect the family. But interrogators who were motivated

to demonstrate their success in creating collaborators marked up many files.
They were paid for that. This is hard to explain in words. It is the worst dirt the
regime did.

From this perspective Mukls' silence surrounding internal fragmentation
is not a silence of denial, but a paralyzing silence connected to their pain.
Despite the political prisoners' knowledge that the StB archives had the same
validity as their arrests and convictions had, these records became the material foundation for exclusion from membership in the Confederation and from
the community of other Mukls. The collective attempt at reconciliation was
partially sabotaged by the release of the state's files. Again political prisoners were silenced and alienated with little more recourse for exoneration than
they had been afforded by the state that initially convicted them.

While the release of StB files has been interrupted, those documents that
have been made available have acquired a central and divisive role in the
recovery process, and the silencing of the political other has extended far
beyond the life of the Communist state. The general desire to make the StB
archive transparent was driven by the strongly held belief in post-socialist
Europe in the power of the written record to provide the truth necessary for
reconciliation.

When I interviewed Gábina, the daughter of a deceased Mukl, she spoke
of the disturbance the released files had caused in her relationship with her
father.

My father once told me about his experience in Pardubice prison and we never
again talked about it. He didn't tell us he had to report to the police regularly.
He lived with a dark cloud in his mind. The fear confined his personhood, and
that was the worst. He had already died when after 1989 his name appeared on
the list of collaborators with the Communist regime. My mother collapsed. She
didn't expect it. I don't know what is the truth. I wish he could be rehabilitated.
Perhaps his record would be clear. When I talked to his best friend, he spoke
with a reserved tone. My father never hurt anyone, he didn't take money, but
he must have been disloyal somehow. His health was damaged. One young
woman, when she learned about her father, committed suicide. I think it was
provocation. They, "Mukls," were the first danger to the old regime. I don't
know what my father would have said, perhaps he would have appealed to the
court-house and once again sought justice.

Gábina, who felt that she had a special silent bond with her father, is
today left with the StB archive legacy. Since her father passed away, it is
she who has to live with her father's files. Because of her fear of facing her
father's choice, as she told me, she has made no attempt to investigate his
files. For Gábina the StB archives continue to be a place of fiction. In this

way Gábina continues to be a subject of the state and its archive in spite
of the post-regime political changes. She continues to live with fear of the
former regime, the construction of her father's Muklhood, and the fictive
character of the StB archive. Thus her father's record is a location and symbol of his moral choice.

The state police archive, in spite of its fictive character, continues to be,
paradoxically, for the Mukls, their relatives and Czech society at large a
place of historical, moral, and ethical truth. The archive, like rumors in the
camps, continues to be a source of internal fragmentation within the Mukls'
community.

In the post-socialist Czech Republic the StB archive retained its centrality,
but in a new context, that of the nation's rehabilitation project. The archives
became the location of political and moral truth about one's record. A "clean"
record was one free of collaboration with the former regime. Ironically, the
political prisoners themselves formed the Confederation of Political Prisoners, and it was they who chose to exclude those who did not have "clean"
records in their individual files. The Confederation established a committee
to examine potential members and excluded those whose files indicated they
had acted as informants or agents.

The archive, as constituted in the present, contributes to the ongoing threat
to Mukl relatedness. Ultimately, even though many Mukls' mutual bonds
were not destroyed by the political fiction, they and their families continue to
live with the consequences of that fiction. I discuss fragmentation as a form
of internal diversity in the Mukls' community as it coexists with solidarity
and belonging to a new family. I point out that for the Mukls, fragmentation
of camaraderie and solidarity was a constant threat.

Communist concentration camps disappeared during the 1960s and early
1970s, but today Mukls return to the places of invisible camps and have in
their remembering reconstructed these spaces. For the Communist regime,
prison was a means of punishment, but for the political prisoners, prison
became a space for the formation of a new community, a new family, a new
home and a new voice. Despite having lived through torture, hard work and
isolation in the prisons, after many years, one of the prisoners, Čeněk in 2002,
expressed his feelings about returning to a former camp as if he is "pulled to
the old and familiar places," as if it was home. Totalitarian prison and camps
were adapted by the Mukls as a home despite boundaries defined by twisted
wire. Within this carved out, isolated territory used as a slave labor camp,
he or she found a home.[23] Mukls' references to prison as a home have to be
understood in the sense of Mukls' comfort with the familiar in contrast to
outside life in a society radically changed since their arrest. While walking
through the transformed landscape, the Mukls', through their remembering,

constructed narratives which are verbal intersections drawn from both the individual and the communal memories of day-to-day life in the camps. They are located in a present time of togetherness in Jáchymov and the other camps to which they return.

Mukls' conversations in Jáchymov, dialogic, never cohesive and unitary, are forms of recovery. For Mukls recovery is the voice recounting the torture of sleep deprivation, hunger, cold; the voice craving one's lover, family or friend; the voice of laughter, magic, and beauty felt with a new family; it is the voice of men whose bodies, coated by uranium dust, survived, returned from hell and went on with a life marked by these tragic encounters. In the Mukls' speech there is loneliness, fragmentation and alienation, just as there is togetherness, relatedness and hope.

Reconciliation, as I observed in the case of Mukls', is among other things the property of communication. Language then is appropriation "which transforms nature into face" (Agamben 2000:90). In the light of reconciliation, "the face is, above all, the passion of revelation, the passion of language" (Agamben 2000:91).

NOTES

1. The country Czechoslovakia was divided in January 1993 into two separate countries: the Czech Republic and Slovakia. In Part II of this book, when I focused on the present conditions of Muklhood and their aging, I limit my discussion to Czechs and the Czech Republic. Throughout this book I also refer to the Czech region as Bohemia. While this term is familiar for outsiders as a common reference to the Czech Republic, Czechs would not refer frequently to the modern Czech Republic as Bohemia. For contemporary Czechs the use of the term *Bohemia* has historical meanings, quite different from how they see the modern Czech Republic.

2. In my discussion of Mukls' mutual relatedness I use the terms *family* and *community* interchangeably. The term *family* is more accurate since that is the way Mukls define themselves. The way they care for each other is closer to their concern for a family member than a friend. When I have used the term *community*, it is based on my own conceptual construct rather than that of the Mukls. Community must be understood in this context as a theoretical tool.

3. Kroča dates the history of mining in Jáchymov to the sixteenth century, when silver mining took place there. Uranium mining began in the nineteenth century, when uranium was used in the production of porcelain glazes. In 1898, the Jáchymov mines became a significant source of radium. During WWII Jáchymov, although occupied by the Germans, was ignored by Hitler. After the war the Soviets made Jáchymov one of the places supplying uranium for the development of atomic weapons (Kroča 2003).

4. Soviets occupied Jáchymov in 1945. For a historical context see Hejl and Kaplan 1986, Kroča 2003, Babka and Veber 2002.

5. *Ostrov* in Czech is "island." Since the Jáchymov camps were managed from the city of Ostrov, located nearby, Mukls compared them to a *gulag* "island" in Russian.

6. For diversity of camp population see the section "Fragmentation" in this chapter.

7. Petrašová states that in 1950 the number of political prisoners in Jáchymov was 11,026; in 1951 it was 15,125; and in 1953 it was 46,675, the largest on record.

8. Petrašová's article is based on archival records in the Central Archive of the Prison Service in Prague, Bory prison in Plzeň, and the Archive of the Minister of the Interior, personal narratives of eight Mukls, and related publications.

9. The year of my visit to Jáchymov, 2003, I encountered approximately three hundred participants. The majority were Mukls who had worked in Jáchymov.

10. The Mukl Confederation of Political Prisoners organizes this annual event. The event is organized and sponsored by the regional chapter of the Confederation. Since 1990 when the first celebration was held, the number of attendees has dramatically declined due to the death or illness of many Mukls.

11. Liquidation in this context is understood as a reference to social invisibility as well as biological death, but not biological genocide such as Nazis' planned liquidations. In Czechoslovakia individual ideological enemies of the state were sentenced to death, but large numbers of Mukls were punished by imprisonment and torture. For a comparative study of different Czechoslovak work camps from 1948 to 1968, see Hejl and Kaplan 1986. For historical documentation of Jáchymov camps see Kaplan and Pacl 1993.

12. I met these Mukls shortly after my arrival at Jáchymov when I was visiting one of the mining sites. I did not know them when we met, but through casual friendly conversation they invited me to join them on their way to see different camps and mining grounds. I followed Jirka, Jarda, and Luboš, and recorded what they told me as well as their conversations. I spent the rest of the day with this group. Jirka came to Jáchymov with his wife, who was fully involved in following the program and conversations. Jiří, who used to work on the rehabilitation committee, was very helpful when I asked questions about rehabilitation and researching crimes of the Communist regime. Luboš and Jarda were just visiting from Switzerland, where they live today as Czech emigrants. Jarda is an illustrator and drew many cartoons on the subject of Mukls and the camps. Later I reconnected with these Mukls in Prague.

13. Novelist Karel Pecka wrote based on the biographical experience of Muklhood. I also refer to Karel Bartošek's interview with Pecka in his book *Czech Prisoners* (Bartošek 2001).

14. Here I use terms from E. E. Evans-Pritchard's writing on time and space in his book, *The Nuer* (E. E. Evans-Pritchard 1940) He, in his description of the Nuer concept of time, distinguished between ecological and structural time. By ecological he means cyclical time in relation to the environment. By structural time he means social and relational time within a social structure.

15. Mukls working in the mines were exposed to uranium dust and as a result suffered from a cough, which they called the laugh.

16. It is historically evident that Czechs have always had, until today, disagreement over their national and cross-national sense of belonging. This fragmentation

among Czechs, over priority of membership, whether first in a Czech nation-state and then in a Europe or a global context, is a subject well documented by historians. For an anthropological perspective see Ladislav Holy 1996 and Ernest Gellner 1994.

17. I have discussed this subject of transformation of relatedness between Mukls and their families and among Mukls themselves in the context of arrest and interrogation in Part II. I am revisiting this subject here in the context of Mukls' remembering their relationships in the camps.

18. See Šimková 1994, Pálkosková-Wiesenbergerová 1991, Bubeníčková-Kuthanová 1991, Šedivý 2002, Ješ 1997, Lesák 2000, Brodský 1971.

19. I have also come across various cartoons and illustrations of life in the work camps. Mukls' drawings of life in the camps depict darkness and cruelty, but some are done in the style of cartoons. Visual representations of Mukls' suffering have a polarity between realistic drawings of darkness in the camps and drawings registering humorous situations and jokes.

20. *Retribuční* refers to a person who was tried or sentenced to prison under the law established after WWII as a means of legalizing the punishment of Nazi sympathizers and collaborators. Babka and Veber (2000) stated that already by the end of May 1945, Czech prisons and existing work camps were filled with Nazis and their sympathizers. Petrašová also noticed that many accusations, often on a local level, of collaboration with Nazis were false and intended to destroy the lives of people who were uncomfortable with emerging political structures. Mukls' testimony about the Nazi prisoners in Jáchymov can be found in Pejskar (Pejskar 1987:208).

21. While governmental anxiety about rumors in India reinforced the colonial making of records of rumors, in the context of the Mukls, rumor was welcomed by the government (in this case the government's power extended to the prison) as a force for the destruction of the Mukls' communal solidarity.

22. An example of such a Mukl's opinion is Jitka M.'s narratives, when she discusses her role on the committee set up to evaluate the political purity of applicants for membership in the Confederation. See references regarding her narratives.

23. The word *community* and its use is not the same as it is in the Czech language. Community is not the word they would use to express their experience of togetherness. Writing in English, I do use the term *community* as a proper expression of Mukls' bonds.

Chapter Six

Beyond Ceremonial Sound

I don't know why I should think that of all one's faculties one would lose one's speech—but that's how it is; perhaps it is because true grief, like true happiness, cannot be encompassed by words.

—Jiří Mucha, from his prison journal

SILENT TOGETHERNESS AND MUKLS' VOICE

Standing next to each other, shaking hands, placing arms around the shoulders of old friends, they silently mourned the dead and celebrated their own survival. In the memorial prayers, speeches, music and marching, all is melded into a single ritual for victims, both living and dead, of the forced labor camps of Jáchymov. Present at the sounds and sights of the memorial are the essentially silent Mukl celebrants. Theirs is the silence of purpose. Some Mukls do not like to speak about their own past, but they do attend the memorials. The phenomenon of formal ceremonial sound and the collective silence of the Mukls marked the annual Saturday ritual in Jáchymov Square. Beyond this ceremonial sound is the silence of survivors whose long-ago tortured bodies, hands, arms, shoulders, faces and thoughts are engaged in these shared moments of togetherness.

On a Saturday morning in May 2003, Mukls[1] gathered in the town square of Jáchymov. This gathering was central to the memorial weekend there. Some attended Mass,[2] others met outside near the sculpture, a memorial to victims and survivors. They came together during the formal, non-religious ceremony on the square by the memorial.[3]

To the public eye the Mukls' unity in Jáchymov Square was a silent political act, an act marking the crimes against them and a protest against the nation's equally silent political act. The event was recorded by a number of TV stations. Before 1989 Mukls were not allowed to gather as a community in public; their forms of individual and communal reconciliation were hidden. The gathering was also one of the opportunities for Mukls to restore their public voice and face through their togetherness and remembering. In Jáchymov they are reclaiming their social visibility through their counter ritual to the state's violent ritual initiated in 1948. Mukls' voice, face, solidarity, survival, and alienation from others are manifested in Jáchymov. The ceremony was followed by a group visit to a memorial in the local cemetery. Then the Mukls separated into small groups for lunch in local restaurants. Some Mukls came only for Saturday morning's ceremony, the visit to the local cemetery, the square gathering, and afterwards for lunch with friends.[4]

In the context of making a Mukl community, I emphasize the voice and face of the political other, which was silenced and defaced by a totalitarian state. I discussed how silencing and lost visibility were integral to the process of forming Mukls' subjectivities. The silence in Jáchymov is no longer the silence in which Mukls' voices are lost; it is an active silence, a silence intended to produce a single and powerful voice. "Suffering is voiceless in the metaphorical sense that silence becomes a sign of something ultimately unknowable" (Morris 1997:27), wrote David Morris in his essay about the literary engagement with the human experience of suffering. And he continued, "Voice matters precisely because suffering remains, to some degree, inaccessible" (Morris 1997:27).

Mukls' silence is one of the forms of register in their language of reconciliation. It expresses their collective unspoken desire for public recognition and acknowledgment. If silence, as Morris informs us, produces a powerful voice expressing what is unknowable of others suffering, then Czech Mukls' silent voice represents a counter voice addressed to those Czechs whose silent voices oppose Mukls' remembering. The state secrecy about violent rituals, as I discussed earlier, produced another kind of silence, public silence. Mukls attribute this silence to the public's loss of memory, as if it is "the denial of pain" (Das 1997:88). The public silence of many other Czechs was confronted by another kind of silence, the silence of the Mukls' remembering.

In conversations Mukls often spoke about the general denial of Communist crimes. Many Mukls perceive that the crimes committed against them in the past are now forgotten; in their view the uncomfortable darkness of the past has been swept away by "collective amnesia" (Das 1997).[5] "The question of memory and representation is not only a question of the authenticity of memory," as Das and Kleinman put it, but it is also the struggle to impose different kinds of truth, creating a past for oneself based on how one deals with the violence of memories in the present (Das and Kleinman 2000:12). The issue of memory becomes a question of the politics of recognition.

Fiona Ross discusses the unfortunate continuity of suffering through memories of violence in interesting ways. In the context of the South African reconciliation project, Ross raised the question of representation of the experience of apartheid and of truth commissions. Ross, like Das, emphasized that silence marks a particular type of knowing, and that silence, if acknowledged, is a legitimate part of the discourse on pain (Ross 2001, Das 1997). Ross, when discussing the struggle to define truth constituted in the aftermath of violence as one of many elements located in reconciliation, and thus different from political truth experienced during the violent acts, emphasized its continuity. Importantly, moral procedures after violence are not about establishing criminal status and determining punishment, but rather are acknowledgments of pain. Such acknowledgments of pain are not limited to individual injuries; they also legitimize the collective quest for repair, revitalization, and healing. What is meant by repair is not just healing, but transformation to a different moral state.

Today many Mukls feel that their suffering is publicly denied. For them the memorials provide opportunities to confront the silence and overcome it. To individuals in search of reconciliation to self, to family and to nation this is vital to the process of their reconciliation.

The struggle for truth continues ever afterwards.

—Ross (2001)

THE RETURN FROM PRISON

I notice how I am losing touch with the world I knew. I remember it, but I feel that it has become different. It seems a little ridiculous to have one's mind filled with useless memories—numbers which no longer mean anything, addresses which no longer exist, and faces which have changed out of recognition. . . . This is what people must feel like when they get old and begin to lose their grip on life. One after another, the links which had tied them to other people are breaking, until their loneliness has become so burdensome that they cease to be afraid of death. It is not so much things or even emotions that I want to stay alive for, but people—and these are now, one by one, vanishing in front of my eyes. (Mucha 1967:213)

For many, return was marked by alienation from a society that changed while they were imprisoned. The 1960s in Czechoslovakia were a time of a loosening of Communist political discipline, in keeping with a global trend. Joseph Stalin and Clement Gottwald, the Czechoslovak president, were both dead. Many political prisoners received presidential amnesties granted by Antonín Zápotocký and were released from work camps. A new generation of Communist leaders such as Dubček and Smrkovský, advocating socialism with a human face, replaced Gottwald's government.[6] Political prisoners began returning home during this time. When they returned, depending on the politics of observers, they were either betrayers or heroes. As a social group in Czechoslovakia, they experienced socialism with a human face, differently than did other citizens. Political prisoners had no place to go, had difficulty finding jobs and felt alienated from their families, friends, and the rest of the country. The state continued to control their lives in a number of different ways. They had to report regularly to their local police station, and the location of their residence was assigned to them. They were caught in the space between the law against unemployment and their unemployability as politicals. Often, they wandered from job to job while trying to remake their personal lives. When I spoke with Mukls about their return, they told me that for many the feeling of social invisibility continued beyond the camp boundaries. This is how Květa, Albína and Jitka talked about return.

> They drove us to the train station after we were set free. We had to go to Prague and register at the police station. I had no place to go. My husband was in prison still. I stayed with my mother and washed dishes at a restaurant. My husband came back, we had a daughter, but then our relationship fell apart. People changed in the prisons. (Květa)
>
> I practically had no place to come back to. I was commanded to stay in Prague. Everybody had to work, unemployment was illegal, but for us the opportunity to work applied only in agriculture, construction, cleaning, and labor. I worked as a cleaning lady in a café. It was night shift. When they found out I was a prisoner, they let me go. The time of return was hard. Nobody from our friends could help us, because they were afraid of us. The apartments the government gave us were in bad condition, with the water and toilets in the hallway. People changed, they were afraid for themselves and their children. (Albína)
>
> After we returned people were afraid of us. In the work place they knew about me. Some people were good to me, but many people kept their distance. I worked as a driver of a tram, later in a restaurant, and later in a hospital. (Jitka)

Those who were released from work camps and prisons were required to report regularly to the police. They remained enemies of the state. Their families remained suspect and continued to be denied rights and privileges accorded to other Czechs. The places to which they returned were for many, if not most, Mukls places where they no longer belonged. Those places and people had been transformed during the Mukls' ten to fifteen years of absence. They discovered that their fellow Czechs seemed to have acquiesced silently to their condition.

To maintain friendships and to express their political solidarity the former political prisoners, forbidden by the state from gathering together, began to organize regular secret meetings. Franta and Roman spoke about their involvement in the organized effort to achieve formal judicial reconciliation.

> When we came home in the sixties, we stayed in touch with friends from prison. Our family and old friends distanced themselves from us. We founded K231 and, with my wife who also came back from prison, I traveled all over the country to build chapters of K231. Later, after '68, the police harassed me because I was in charge of the K231 archive. (Franta M)
>
> I worked in the mines (uranium mines) and was stuck there until the sixties. I got involved in K231. All my friends told me to leave the country, you are an adventurer, but they left and I stayed. My mother was waiting for me; my wife was not well. My wife died and I had to raise my daughter by myself. (Roman)

For many Mukls returning to their family and society meant not only leaving what had become a new home and new family, but also as Roman said, "a life of unusual intensity." After many years of imprisonment, they had not only adapted to life as a socially isolated group but had also enjoyed, within that group, camaraderie and intellectual stimulation. Mukls valued the opportunity to meet a variety of different people of different professional backgrounds in the prisons. They often emphasized their personal intellectual and spiritual growth during their time in prison. In the prisons they found spiritual and intellectual leaders. In retrospect, they cherished this opportunity, as they believe it would not otherwise have been possible. Among the imprisoned were the Czechoslovak intellectual elite, spiritual leaders, men and women from different religious orders,[7] writers, scientists and university professors. All of them shared their knowledge with the other prisoners. The prison lectures in art history by Dr. Komárková are not only remembered by Muklyně but also were published and widely distributed. I discuss fragmentation as a form of internal diversity in the Mukls' community as it coexists with solidarity and belonging to a new family. I point out that for the Mukls, fragmentation of camaraderie and solidarity was a constant threat. Priests and members of religious orders were tortured brutally in prisons, and yet are remembered by many as spiritual leaders, despite their having had limited contact with others.

Before returning home some prisoners planned the organization K231. This organization for political prisoners, established to rehabilitate Mukls, was founded in the late 1960s and was the first attempt by Mukls to recover their lost voice. Mukls had planned on reclaiming their voice and social face within the rehabilitation process (Kmet 1972). Their effort was interrupted by the Soviet armed invasion of August 1968. The organization K231 went underground and resurfaced in 1989 as the Confederation of Political Prisoners.

During the summer of 2005, when visiting with my parents, my father pulled out a collection of essays written and self-published, under a pseudonym, by a Mukl friend of his, now deceased. In this collection of short stories, one story stood out, a biographical story titled "Luděk." This story is about a Mukls' return from prison. In the train on his way home, prisoner Luděk is asking himself questions about the changes in his home with his children and his wife while he was away. He is not sure what the children will say to him upon his return after such a long time. He is questioning his return; to him eight years is such a long time. He thinks about his wife and how "inconvenient" his return will be for her since she is pregnant now by somebody else. In the story Luděk's senses intersect with the rhythm of the train. "The wheels on the train are making the powerful pounding of laughter.". . . "But he was, after all, in prison and eight years is a long time for a healthy woman to wait. What does it matter that she had two kids with Luděk? One idea is chasing the other; the pounding wheels are more and more powerful" (Kmet 1972). Then he arrives and even his brother is surprised by his return. The brother is explaining that he cannot go home, but Luděk understood this for a long time. His strongest desire is to see his children, but he doubts how he will handle the emotional intensity of such a big reunion. When he sees his children that evening he sings the song he wrote for them in prison: "When one day again, your daddy returns, back to his little girl, he will stroke, he will kiss her hair, he will enjoy again the whole world" (Kmet 1972). His wife divorced him while he was in prison and the children are in her custody, so he has to be satisfied when they come to see him sometimes. Yes, he finds another possibility, that no one knows about; he comes to see his children secretly, from outside through the window when they go to bed. This is as happy as Mukl Luděk will be after his return.

Reading this story I realized that not only did I remember Luděk from the past, but I also knew his first wife, children and her new husband, the one she meet when Luděk was in prison. In my memory her new husband was an old drunk and I would see him every night wobbling home in the late night hours. At some point my parents had a dog that barked at him every time he was passing. From inside our house, without looking, we could tell it was he staggering by. This daily passage is stuck in my childhood memory, but until that summer, I was not aware of all these connections. I did not know that the drunk's wife who lived up on the hill was Luděk's first wife. She was always looking troubled, and her family seemed fragmented and problematic.

On reflection, this story reminds me of the silences surrounding our daily lives during socialism. Even if our parents knew something, they often could not explain it all. That silence was born from fear, or a sense of protection or their denial.

Beyond my own personal connection, Luděk's text carries a rich register of prisoners' emotional and material experiences upon their returns. It conveys the feelings of betrayal, alienation and social death as a consequence of imprisonment, which all Mukls faced upon their return. They felt betrayed and isolated, a feeling they all shared. Albína published a memoir in which she wrote how she shared this experience of alienation with her Muklyně friend from prison: "When Jiřina and I meet there is no need for us to talk, just looking from eyes to eyes, and she and I know. Our eyes said: 'What else were you expecting?' This was clear already in prison" (Pálkosková-Weisenbergová 1981:85).

A Mukl's return is also remembered clearly by their relatives. They too seemed to feel alienated from the Mukl for whom many of them waited. The relatives of Mukls, as I wrote elsewhere, also lived in isolation. They were also marked by the state as dangerous because of their kinship with Mukls. For them the return was a significant and tension-filled moment. They often suffered with Mukls, but as they expressed, Muklhood was hard to understand for those who had not shared the experience. In the summer of 2003, the wife of one Mukl said,

> It was the 9th of May celebrations when I learned about the amnesties. I went to see my girlfriend, with whom I was close. Her husband was a fellow prisoner with my husband. She was also a mother with one boy and I had two. We shared our feelings during the time that our husbands were arrested, we developed a nice friendship. I had no hope of my husband returning, but he came. I was at my work, so I walked home. I wanted him to tell me about his life in the prison, but he said, "I am sorry I can't; I am not up to it; maybe some day."

Family members outside of the prison who waited for lost relatives suffered a loss of hope for a return, and they suffered from not knowing about life in prison, the experience Mukls found impossible to communicate. The absence of available language immediately after the return from prison made it impossible for many to speak about their passage, the journey to Muklhood. Silence was protecting them from greater pain; they were suffering from post-traumatic stress. I came across testimonies about Mukls' mutual closeness and strong friendships, described by Albína, when I was searching for Mukls' relatives, the compassionate outsiders to Muklhood. One of the wives spoke about an episode shortly after her husband returned.

One evening I remember, I came home from work, opened the door, and was in a state of shock, the whole room was full of Mukls. Imagine! They sat everywhere, in the kitchen, on the chairs, sofa, floor. It was spectacular, they were talking, they seemed to me as if from a different world; they were men and they were hugging, kissing, holding hands, crying, laughing, that was an experience that no normal person (one who has not experienced such a fate) can have; it was beautiful!

The experiences of prison followed by alienation after release were powerful foundations for the personal friendships and connectedness that evolved. Their need to stay in touch and to exercise expressions of solidarity are evident in their words, as well as the words of others. Their relationships, formed in prison, continued as personal friendships and political belonging, membership in the Mukls' newly established organization, K231. After their return, while alienated from their own families, husbands, wives, children and others, many Mukls maintained the bonds formed in prison. Shared suffering in camps and prisons shaped a new kind of relatedness, one that formed the basis of political solidarity and of personal closeness. This friendship or kinship emerging was one of the most significant features of Muklhood that reached beyond the boundaries of prison. In spite of all they had lost, many Mukls shared a deep sense of belonging to a new family.

After their return, many could not easily speak about life in the prisons. The Mukls' silence reinforced the secrecy surrounding Muklhood. That silence was alienating for both Mukls and non-Mukls. While Mukls' returns from prison interrupted one form of isolation and denial of voice, it immediately produced a new set of historical circumstances under which Mukls' voices continued to be denied. Mukls' secret meetings after prison and their continued camaraderie were important to them. Establishing the relationship among Mukls, Czech society and the political power dominant at the moment of their return is important for understanding their continued alienation and also for some recent forms of reconciliation.

The Jáchymov event, as I conceptualized it, is one of the Mukls' ways of reconciling.[8] I have interpreted Mukls' participation in Jáchymov as their active restoration of those moments when speech, representing agency, had been denied.[9] The restlessness within the Mukls' language of reconciliation is provoked by "that moment in history, when there is no language" (Agar 1994:205). While developing new language, Mukls are making "available discourse for conversation" (Agar 1994:205). In Agar's words: "the walls around talk," broken down from the outside, by revolution in 1989, are now being broken down from the inside by the Mukls. The forbidden topic, Muklhood, is now becoming the new discourse, and it requires a new framework, a new social fact, for the Mukls' "languaculture" (Agar 1994, Goffman 1974).

The narratives about Muklhood are subjected to the contexts in which they are constructed, but the pain of trauma endures into the next generation. The children of Mukls I interviewed also revealed that Muklhood has significantly marked their relationships to their parents in spite of the parents' efforts to hide their burden. While Mukls are defining a new language to communicate their condition, their children are engaged in defining their own language of reconciliation as well.

CLAIMING JUDICIAL SPACE

After the trial, the face of the political other disappeared and remained invisible to Czech society until the 1960s. When prisoners returned, many in 1961 or later, from the camps and prisons to their families, homes and workplaces, many of them were called for years afterward for regular or random visits to the police station. For some, harassment by the police did not stop until 1989 when the Communist government collapsed and the political system changed. However, a legacy from the previous regime lives on. The quest for legal justice continues to be an integral part of Mukls' life in post-Communist Czech Republic.

They seek recognition of their suffering. From their perspective, this recognition should take place in the courtrooms, the same courtrooms where Mukls' voices were muted by judges during the Monster Trials in the 1950s. Despite their earlier experience with Czechoslovak law, they turned with hope towards the judicial institutions and asked the court system for rehabilitation. They seek justice for the punishment of injustices committed by individual agents. In this section I will discuss this dilemma, which was made clear to me through the events that took place during the weekend memorial gathering in Jáchymov.

Late on a Saturday afternoon, in May 2003, over one hundred people met in the Jáchymov movie theater for the open forum. This forum is a significant part of the Mukls' annual memorial celebration. It lasted for over two hours and, like the morning gathering on the square, was filmed by Czech Public TV and an independent documentary filmmaker, Kristína Vlachová.[10]

This gathering was coordinated from the podium by five Mukls, all members of the Confederation of Political Prisoners. Each of the five presented a different issue, and then opened the discussion to the entire forum. One of the central subjects discussed at the forum in 2003 was the enforcement of laws relating to crimes committed against prisoners between 1948 and 1989. After 1989, some Mukls politically engaged the Czech Senate to approve a new law that would enforce legal action against individuals who had committed crimes during the

Communist regime. One of the Mukls involved in this process spoke at the forum from the podium:

Mukl speaker 1: Dear friends, we can't expect a Nuremberg trial, that is impossible today in this context, but as long as the crimes of communism remain untried morally, this state will remain an illegal state. I was deeply invested in the process, unfortunately, and we all know it, we have inherited a judicial system from the previous regime.

Mukl from audience: It is clear that the criminals are not only living today among us, but they have special privileges as well.

Mukl speaker 1: The problem that we run into is presidential amnesties. The president has the right to give amnesty, but unfortunately the amnesty given by the president is giving freedom to these criminals. When I applied with a proposal for investigating and punishing for the criminal act of killing, the judge qualified the case, as they often do, as misconduct on the job, in which case it is covered by amnesty from the 1960s.

Mukl from audience: The legal system didn't change, the actors just changed their positions, judges and prosecutors, and others working there shifted around, and now they can continue. . . .

Mukl speaker 2: I was after them, but it is not my fault that the judicial system maintains this continuity.

Mukl speaker 1: Dear friends, in terms of statistics we are still first in punishing the crimes compared to Germans, Hungarians, Poles and Slovenians. But, for example, in Slovenia, a judge involved in the previous regime can't continue serving today.

Mukl from audience: We don't say somebody must be destroyed, but until the evil is punished we have to meet.

Mukl speaker 1: You all know that I protested against judicial nonacceptance of crimes under communism. I think our chance is in the European Union. That is why we have to vote for membership. That is the only way this state will be forced to become legal!

Mukl from audience: Just remember the Lukeš case—today he is dead.

From the meeting it is evident how Mukls are frustrated with the legal institutions unchanged after the fall of socialism. Some Mukls, still very active considering their age, entered the new political scene with the hope of accomplishing major changes, especially in the area of the corrupted legal system. When Mukls discussed specific problems with the process of rehabilitation, they referred to the Lukeš case. I learned about Mukl Lukeš later from a documentary film made by Vlachová, whom I met at the forum. Her films are based on individual narratives, mostly those of Mukls, though she also made a film about a former guard. In one of her films she documented the case of Lukeš.

In the first part of the film Lukeš verbally reconstructed what happened in the prison. He had escaped and as he was running, a guard in a tower shot him. Lukeš collapsed, and after the guard caught up with him he again shot him several times from behind. A number of guards all clustered over Lukeš, and when a second guard indicated an intention to shoot him yet again the others stopped him. Lukeš survived the shooting, left prison in the 1960s, returned home, married and had a number of children. After the fall of the Communist regime in 1989 Lukeš sought, and was granted, a reinvestigation of his case.

In the second part of the film the guard, now accused of a criminal act, is interviewed. He is filmed at home with his wife in the background. He denied any criminal behavior. On the contrary, he talked about how good things were for prisoners in the camps. "They had enough money to buy many things, such as salami and other food."

After Lukeš's first appeal at the regional level the judge found in his favor and the guard was sentenced to three years in prison. The guard appealed to a higher court. The final part of the film was shot in the courtroom where the appeal was heard. The judge heard the case, invited Lukeš to state his case and then allowed the guard to present his defense. The guard's argument was centered on the fact that he was just an employee of the prison, and he acted under conditions dictated by his work duty. "The prisoner was running towards the forbidden zone in the camp, and my duty as a guard was to shoot. There was a sign stating forbidden entry, and Mr. Lukeš, violated this rule." In the judge's response, one question stood out, "Mister Lukeš did you see the sign indicating forbidden entry, and did you violate such a rule?" In the film, after the judge's question, silence fell over the room. I think it was a moment of disbelief that the judge could ask such a question. In the end the guard was released. A few months later, Lukeš died and the case was closed. Reconciliation within the judicial system never happened for Lukeš.

The Lukeš case remains unresolved in the Mukls' view, and it is for many Mukls a point of reference when they talk about justice. It also represents other unresolved cases. The Institute for the Investigation of the Crimes of the Communist Regime,[11] which I visited several times in 2004, contains archival materials of all investigations conducted by the Institute after 1989. It also retains incomplete rehabilitation files from the 1960s. As it was explained to me, the process of an investigation is initiated by a Mukl's request. Each case then is routinely evaluated by three different groups of Institute employees, historians, detectives, and lawyers. The historians and detectives investigate the case and produce documentation; a lawyer then has to make a decision as to whether, according to the law, the case should be presented to the courts. I learned, based on my conversations with one of the historians[12] working in the Institute, that in many cases the lawyer stopped the process before the case could get to the courtroom. Since 1989 many Mukls have also appealed directly to the court, but often, legal pursuit of crimes committed by state police and prison camp employees is a long and slow process.

The forum is an event during which everyday fears from the past and desired hopes for the future are brought to light. In their speech Mukls raise their voice for acknowledging the crimes of the past. At the forum the prosecutors, the judges, the workers, the secret policemen, the torturers and the camp guards are called upon to admit their participation in the crimes against Mukls. At the forum the Mukls' speech registers their desire for justice. Justice is still the Mukls' place of hope.

Mukls' speech at the forum is a critique of the state's and the justice system's silence about the crimes of the Communist regime, of the continuity of legal texts, of the comfort of torturers, and of the disconnectedness of judges. Mukls' voices are asking, not for revenge, but for moral acknowledgment of their losses under the Communist regime. Mukls see the politics of continuity as marked by "collective amnesia" (Das 1997). Historian Jacques Rupnik has characterized the post-1989 era as the time of "the post-totalitarian blues" during which the "double political game is the split between continuity and radical change" (Rupnik 1995: 62).

Historically, social and political life in 1950s Czechoslovakia was overshadowed by the events of 1968 and the era of the dissident movement during the 1970s and 1980s. These events, much more than the repression and its victims, have become the heart of the story being told. During informal conversations at Ganys, Mukls express deep distrust of legal institutions and often acknowledge that the court does not grant them any opportunity for recovering. In their conversations, the legal process is the only way they see to regain their lost voice and face. When discussing this subject at Ganys, several of the Mukls put it this way:

Mukl 1: Until we have legal ways to acknowledge that we were wrongly accused of criminal acts, this state is not a legal state, and we haven't got democracy.

Mukl 2: Today amnesia concerning the severe political crimes of the Communist era is widespread in Czech. In the eyes of the young generation it is forgotten history.

Mukl 3: They can't understand and there is no possibility of sharing the experience. They have an unwillingness to recognize the crimes. Just remember the Lukeš case. And it is one of a number of unresolved cases.

Mukl 1: Legal continuity is at the core of the problem. Laws protecting the totalitarian state's acts are still, today, considered as legal protection of the criminal acts of the state against its citizens from the Communist period.

From the Mukls' perspective the legal system failed to protect them in 1948, and it is failing to reclaim their legal rights after 1989. They imagined that rehabilitation would take place in a courtroom. Despite their experience with the absence of justice within a judicial system that conformed to state ideology rather than serve the citizens, they continue returning to the state's judicial institutions, pleading for the court to acknowledge publicly the mistake and the fictive character of the 1948 defacement. From the perspective of many Mukls, failure of the post-Communist judicial system to review the legal texts and judges' interpretations from the period after 1948 has served to maintain legal continuity with that past. For Mukls this means continuity of injustice. Mukls are up against what Agamben pointed out in the context of camps.

> The correct question regarding the horrors committed in the camps, therefore, is not the question that asks hypocritically how it could have been possible to commit such atrocious horrors against other human beings; it would be more honest, and above all more useful, to investigate carefully how—that is, thanks to what juridical procedures and political devices—human beings could have been so completely deprived of their rights and prerogatives to the point that committing any act toward them would no longer appear as a crime (at this point, in fact, truly anything had become possible). (Agamben 2000)

For the Mukls the politics of continuity are not acceptable strategies for remaking life after terror. They argue for the politics of recognition when "remaking political life" (Das 1997) after the fall of the Communist government. Mukls' politics of discontinuity are embodied in their pursuit of public recognition. In many Mukls' eyes, the Czech nation, when voting for membership in the European Union, is hoping for freedom[13] and also hoping to forget its own past[14] (Pehe 2002, Rupnik 1995). But Mukls' desired freedom is reconciliation, and they pursue it through the possibility of return to a courtroom, thus creating a symbiosis between the language of pain and judicial language. Ironically, legal discourse is the Mukls' desired location for marking the crimes of the Communist regime. The Mukls' experience of betrayal by the Czechoslovakian justice system and their awareness of the circumstances under which the StB archive was made did not change their belief in a moral legal state. Their hope is invested in justice within the legal morality of the state. The courtroom, where they were marked as enemies of their people, where the constructed fiction of their lives was legalized, is the place where they hope to be publicly exonerated or liberated. In spite of the Mukls' experience with the failure of judicial institutions to protect its citizens and promote justice, justice meted out in the courtroom is the hope of many Mukls' today. The ethics of political life have proved that the ethics of law are crucial to the Mukls in their effort towards reconciliation. Their politics today embody their efforts to recover their voice and face and reflect the continuity of the consequences of becoming a Mukl.

READING THE FACE

Reading face and recovering face from the past were my points of entry for this case study. I expressed how relevant it had been for me when I returned to the Czech Republic to read first the faces of the people in the Prague streets, and then the Mukls' faces at Café Ganys. This became the first field data I collected. Although collecting the individual testimonies and analyzing data took me in several different directions, all related to the formation of subjectivity, the subject of face remained important. Face remained for me a location within which one's internal self is communicated to the external world. I recalled Agamben's point, that appearance becomes "the location of a struggle for truth" and that face is "above all, the passion of revelation" (Agamben 2000:91). In fact, face and language possess for Agamben the contradictory power between being the place of opening and communicability (Agamben 2000:91). "What face exposes and reveals is not something that could be formulated as a signifying proposition of sorts, nor is it a secret doomed to remain forever incommunicable" (Agamben 2000:91). Reading facial features means entering the zone of human communicability. The face is an essential expression of human experience. For Taussig, as he refers to Levinas's and Nietzsche's philosophy of face, crossing back and forth between mask and window to the soul is a necessary human task. This stretch of limits, as he called it, gives the face infinity. Face is flexible in the sense that it can be transformed from a mask to a window to the soul (Taussig 1999:224). This function of face creates a paradox; face can never exist alone. Face can only be face when faced by another face (Taussig 1999:225).

In my photographs, the face, photographic portraits of former prisoners, takes on its own expressive power in the act of recovering or reclaiming its location in the public eye. I regard my photographs in this book, portraits of political prisoners, as a way to think about restoring language, hence face, to people, to political prisoners, who have been muted or defaced. By looking closely into prisoners' individual faces and listening to their voices, I hope to read how they negotiated their way through the state violent acts. I aim to show the complexity of lives lived under a violent, totalitarian political system in Central Eastern Europe.

In Jáchymov and during returns to other camps and prisons, Mukls are recovering their face, a symbolic location of their tragic truth. Giorgio Agamben defined face:

> The face is at once the irreparable being—exposed of humans and the very opening in which they hide and stay hidden. The face is the only location of community, the only possible city. And that is because that which in single individuals opens up to the political is the tragicomedy of truth, in which they always already fall and out of which they have to find a way. (Agamben 2000:90)

Valentine Daniel, in writing on violence in Sri Lanka, told the story of a woman he had interviewed in a refugee camp. She had lost her son in an army raid five years earlier. She later lost all her photographs of the son when a helicopter gunship dropped a gasoline bomb on her house. In her narratives she said that though she remembers a lot from his life, she could not recall his face. The face of her son was lost in her memory. Daniel wrote that "this did not prevent her from seeing her son in the face of every young man who came to the camp" and "the traces of her son's face appeared and disappeared in all of them" (Daniel 1997:337). This narrative brings to our attention the way memory and vision are interconnected within the process of coping with loss due to violent events. In this case, remembering the face is an effort to remake a lost image.

Photographer Sebastio Salgado in writing about his own documentary work said that when he documented refugees from around the world, the misplaced, the people affected by wars, genocides, and natural disasters, children always appeared around him and then followed him. Finally he said, "I am going to sit here. If you want me to take a picture of you, line up and I'll take a picture of you" (Salgado 2000:7). Salgado made portraits of children and wrote:

> Children who had been laughing and shouting only seconds earlier were suddenly serious. The noisy crowd had become individuals who, through their clothes, their poses, their expressions and their eyes, were telling stories with disarming frankness and dignity. Through their candid expressions, the sadness and suffering they had known in their short lives was poignantly apparent. (Salgado 2000:8)

Salgado reveals how making the portraits of surviving children transformed them into storytellers, and how their faces revealed their dignity to him. I recognized the Mukls' return to Jáchymov as a language of reconciliation, through which Mukls reclaim their dignity, their lost face. In Jáchymov Mukls are making their experiences known. Whether they return and reconstruct their pasts through their narratives in the camps, or gather in Jáchymov Square for the formal celebration, they are reclaiming their voices and faces through silent togetherness and expressing their communal struggle to recover the truth about their experiences of violence in the past. Their language of reconciliation is the property of individuals as well as the property of the Mukls' community.

Mukls or Muklyněs, the subjects of public defacement, struggle to find a way to tell their stories. Their defacement was an act of public denial of visibility, of face. While passing through the space of death, the process of defacement, a Mukl was subjected to the labor of being made invisible. During trial, a public defacement finalized the Mukl's loss of face. Publicly shamed by the state as a political other, his visibility was unwelcome to the political establishment and its sympathizers. The Mukl's sense of vision was controlled, as was his visibility to the public. Acknowledging Mukls' visual patterns and the role of vision in relation to violence allows us to see what Mukls' politics are today. Their efforts to recover lost visibility during their memorial rituals have been supported by the Czech media. Both television and radio broadcast some of their events and have produced documentary programs about Mukls. The presence of the media in the 1950s, and now after 1989, has raised questions about the role of the media in the context of Muklhood.

In the 1950s the media was in the hands of the Communist Party and produced extensive film documents from the Trials. Radio was used to poison the masses against political others, to strategically agitate and mobilize the Czechoslovak public. Media in Czechoslovakia not only assisted with defacement, but also clearly served the state from 1948 until 1989. The state, led by the Communist Party, made media an effective vehicle for propagandizing its ideology.

The media work since 1989, documenting Mukls' events and producing documentary films about Muklhood, has established a new form of archive, a counter archive to that of the StB. The archive, in Foucault's perspective, is the location of "discursive formation" (Foucault 1972) where knowledge, time and histories intersected. From the perspective of Mukls, the archive is the constitution of their subjectivity as a form of knowledge, a place where information is stored and recalled.

In anthropological practice the archival processes have always occupied a central place. Whether it is a matter of the literal recording that takes the place in field notes, whether it is visual records, or as the site of the production of knowledge, anthropologists have a critical interest in how information is stored and recalled. In this book I discuss how various forms of archival production, as well as the state of the media, impacted Mukls' subjectivities. Taking into account issues such as the function of violence in the events of defacement and everyday matters of justice and morality in conflict recovery, I reflect here on my visual and written configurations.

I began with photographs of individual Mukls' faces and individual life stories. I was moving back and forth between the visual and the written. The visual representation is as important an expression of Muklhood as is the written analysis. To me a camera is an epistemological tool in this project, not just a mechanical means of reproducing images. Picturing, as "visual knowing" (Ruby 2000) in the tradition of observational photography and cinema in anthropology, is based on picture makers translating reality to a visual argument or impression (Banks and Morphy 1999). Visual discourse today involves picturing a moment on an experiential level. Photographing and filming have become, in a broad sense, part of experiencing. No longer just memorializing, the recording of extraordinary events, taking or a matter of staged studio style picture taking, or the domain of trained professionals and amateurs, photographing and filming is part of life experiencing. But, as Susan Sontag's writing regarding the torturing of others reminds us, taking pictures has become part of our normality, even when it comes to photographing or filming when torturing and then sharing it on the Internet (see Sontag 2004). This leads to questions about archival productions. How is the most recent Mukls' archive, then, positioned in this new visual discourse?

I have taken the concept of face as a dialogic means for me to describe and participate in ethical and moral issues. I think of face as recognition of the archive, but also as facing the archive. For me, it is the task of dialogic representation, recognition, and identification to convey the notion of face as it relates to Muklhood. It is also my own facing of individual and collective voice and body, matters of truth, and historicity. My reading of face is what Taussig called "refacement" (Taussig 1999:249). My participation in rites of counter defacement aims to recover previously state-defaced Mukls' faces. If face is evidence, as Taussig suggested, my portraits are counter evidence to that fictive evidence which prisoners were forced to acknowledge during their trials as proof of guilt. In pursuing the theory of subject as a conceptual tool of my analysis, I hope my portraits of Mukls will convey face reading as an act of recovering lost face, an act of visual reconciliation.

On the global map the remaking of life after political violence takes different forms. On the outskirts of a Guatemalan city poor women make angels of hope, while in the Guatemalan highlands women sew quilts from fabric imprinted with the faces of slain relatives. In El Mozote, El Salvadoran people rebury the bodies of the massacred. In South Africa victims give testimony to the reconciliation committee. In Rwanda, Argentina, Peru, the former Yugoslavia, Ireland, India, Sri Lanka, Afghanistan, the former Soviet Union, the effort to come to terms with the experienced political violence is inseparable from the present time. In the Czech Republic, Mukls, who are returning to the places of their Hells to remember, relate, and reclaim, are continuing to develop their language of reconciliation and hoping to recover their voice and face.

NOTES

1. In 2003 there were approximately four hundred people, the majority of them Mukls and Muklyněs, plus relatives, local Jáchymov residents, and a small group of Czech politicians. The Confederation of Political Prisoners, in particular the chapter located in the Czech city of Karlovy Vary, organized this event, like the rest of the Jáchymov celebration. There are no sponsors other than the Mukls themselves, as I learned from a Mukl who is a member of the administration in the Confederation.

2. Mass was celebrated by a Mukl priest and bishop in the Catholic Church on the square.

3. The following day, Saturday, I met Franta and Roman from the Ganys group on the Jáchymov town square, and spent the rest of the day with them.

4. During the morning ceremony, I connected with two Mukl friends, Franta and Roman, and later joined them for lunch. After lunch, I went to the final Mukls' event in Jáchymov, a gathering in a local movie theater for the open forum.

5. During my fieldwork in 2003, I asked an additional research question, What is the relationship between Muklhood today and public discourse? I have initiated several meetings with scholars concerned with recent Czech history and politics. I have met with Jiří Pehe, Jacques Rupnik, and Oldřich Tůma and discussed with them questions regarding public discourse and Mukls' reconciliation today. These conversations were helpful for my conceptual perspective on the relationship between the Mukls' community and Czech society at large.

6. For more on historical context see Kaplan 1990, Pithart 1990, and Rupnik 2002.

7. Of all those arrested, men and women from religious orders and clergy suffered most. According to Mukls' testimonies many were tortured nearly to death or until their lives ended. See Václav Vaško 1990 and 1999.

8. Following the Subaltern Group, I have conceptualized the annual event in Jáchymov as a historical moment through which Mukls can speak, "a moment of active defiance" (Guha 1988, Pandey 1997, 2000, Amin 1995).

9. My earlier reading of the Subaltern Group has influenced my discussion of Mukls' voice. In particular Guha's essay "Chandra's Death" (Guha 1999), which concerns moments of historical denial of speech, has been formative for my understanding of the notion of voice.

10. Kristína Vlachová is a Czech filmmaker, one of the most active in producing documentary films about Mukls.

11. I originally planned to study in depth the documents in this institution. On my first visit, I read older documentation filed from the period between 1967 and 1968. When I returned the following week, the files that I had studied were not available. I realized that the secrecy surrounding this institution would not allow me to work with documents in a systematic way. Based on that, I decided not to use such data and discontinued my work there.

12. The historian wished not to be identified by name.

13. For a political-historical analysis of Czech discourse see Pehe 2002 and Rupnik 1995.

14. During the process of Czech integration into the European Union, the question of recovery from the past was one of the critical points of public discourse (Pehe 2002).

Chapter Seven

Last Visit

A Mukl's moment of morning awakening may be marred by nightmares from the previous night. For many individual Mukls, their own everyday reconciliation begins with facing the morning. In the absence of a community of others with the same or similar experiences, these awakenings often reinforce their sense of isolation. Their ordinary lives, day-to-day conditions, are marked by witnessing or experiencing health problems, serious illness, aging and death. Today, Mukls are part of the oldest generation living in the Czech Republic. In the context of day-to-day life they live on the edge of society. They are retired from work, and although many participate in their families by helping their children, grandchildren, or other relatives, or in taking care of their Mukl friends, others are alone. Among those whom I know well, I have observed that the ones who connect with other Mukls have the richest friendships. During my extended visits to the Czech Republic, between 2003 and 2005, I observed friendships among Mukls in various small groups. The contact I kept with Franta, Čeněk, Roman, and Vojta made it possible for me to see their friendship in a day-to-day context.

It was my last Sunday in Ganys, in the summer of 2005, when I was with a small group of Mukls, Franta, Roman and Vojta, the last of the survivors. At noon all the church bells in Prague center rang out. I stepped out of our conversation to listen to the bells and then shared with the Mukls how much I had forgotten about the rhythm of this city. After a short silence, one of the men responded, "That is what I heard when arrested. In the dark cell, near by Malostranské Náměstí (Lesser Town Square), naked and hungry for days, all I could hear was the sound of bells and barking dogs." This was a reminder for me of how much I focused on the extraordinary, the events from the past or present. In the last chapter of this book, in an attempt to give a sense of the ordinary life of Mukls, how they live their lives now, I will present the visit of Franta, Roman and Vojta to see Čeněk in the hospital. I will present this fragment from the ordinary as evidence of the connectedness embodied in a Mukl's day, through which some aspects of lived Muklhood become evident.

ČENĚK'S SONG

Čeněk now lives in the hospital. His friends know he is dying. After a Mukls' meeting at the café, I went to visit him. On the way to the hospital they joked.

Vojta: I will go to his room first. You wait downstairs, and I'll tell him that he got the death sentence and the police are here. We'll surprise him.

Franta: You will see, he lost a lot of weight, but he still enjoys his bourbon and cigarette.

Vojta: I visit him regularly and bring him his little medicine, which is his last pleasure. He lost his wife, and after that his health went down. He has a daughter; she is busy with her life. His body is giving up on him.

Franta: He was the one who composed our Mukls' hymn. Do you know it?

Jana: Yes, but if you'd sing it to me again, I'd appreciate it.

The Mukls are singing their hymn, a song composed by Čeněk in prison. Their voices fill the interior of the car with a melody symbolic of Muklhood. I am absorbing the song, but also still thinking about their way of joking. Mukls' joking is surprising; it is a sudden language switch, just like this conversation in the car. Vojta's plan to joke with Čeněk is a performative re-enactment of Čeněk's sentence. Forty years ago, Čeněk was sentenced to death by the Communist government. His punishment was changed to life in prison and he survived. Now his friends, Mukls who care for him, remind him through language play of his closeness to death in the past. Alfred Radcliffe-Brown in the Durkheim and Mauss tradition discussed "joking relations" in the context of kinship studies. Joking relations permitted or as required by custom function as a mechanism for the readjustment of the social structure in the case of structural change. Joking then is a functional system for maintaining solidarity and cohesion in society and limiting social conflicts.

Joking, permitted in Mukls' relations, became an available form of speech in the camps, a place of new social structures. But joking relations also play a significant role in the process of remembering in a time of reconciliation. Remembering joking from the camps brings up pleasant memories, and joking while remembering makes remembering pleasant.

We approached the hospital parking lot. Motol Hospital is a modern hospital built on the outskirts of Prague. Numerous high rises are spread over expansive hospital grounds connected by asphalt roads. The whole place evokes the sense of a satellite city extending outward from Prague's center city neighborhoods.

Vojta and I entered the hospital and walked towards Čeněk's room. There was no security guard to stop us. We could freely walk into this building and continue through the hallway until we found Čeněk's room. The interiors are typical of modern hospital architecture in Czech Republic. Hallways and rooms have low ceilings and large windows, and are generally not spacious. Patients always have to share a room with other patients. Small rooms and even hallways in Czech hospitals are often overheated when compared to American hospitals that seem to me always overly air-conditioned. Čeněk is in intensive care in the room he shares with several older men. Čeněk, in his nightgown, sits on a chair with a small desk attached. When we entered he was finishing his lunch. Vojta offered to help him get dressed and then take him out to the front of the hospital, where we could sit on a bench and talk.

As we waited for them, I thought about life in old age and how quickly a human body can change in a year. Last year Čeněk and I had gone to art exhibitions. We walked through the center of Prague, drank wine and talked about art, a life interest he never lost. Now I am in the hospital parking lot waiting for him to come out.

Čeněk, wrapped in a robe, sat in the wheelchair pushed by his friend Vojta. The Čeněk I know is an intellectual, a poet and lover of art. Our conversations have always been interwoven with his slightly cynical sense of humor. It was a kind of humor that he shared with many Mukls, full of irony, even harshness, but never bitter. Čeněk's body was trapped in the wheelchair; the body that was once under arrest, tortured, isolated, intended to be liquidated, but that survived, is now imprisoned once again by its own diminishing vitality. Vojta poured him a small shot of bourbon and lit his cigarette. He served him with kindness and tenderness. Čeněk's face was transformed the moment he inhaled his cigarette and began the conversation.

I read in his face his continuing ability to focus his mind and his strength to express thoughts and ideas reflecting both the past and the present. It was as though his mind could never rest from Muklhood. His intellectual energy fought his body. As an exile, Muklhood had become his habitus, a condition he shares with other Mukls.

In the hospital parking lot I found myself in the middle of a Mukls' social event, an event marking what Mukls have become today. Franta and Vojta's visit to the hospital is an act of Mukl solidarity, caring for a friend. Taking care of a friend is for Franta and Vojta also an act directed towards the other Mukls with whom they share pain. Vojta networks constantly to help those who are ill or who have other life difficulties, visiting them, making food for them, taking them treats, like Čeněk's cigarettes, making sure their health needs are being met.

Franta, with who I am in touch, is involved in caring for other Mukls. During our telephone calls, I always ask Franta about his "today." It often revolves around helping Mukls and their families. In addition to the annual memorial gatherings of the Confederation, Mukls often connect with one another for gatherings such as regular visits for chitchats, hospital visits, and celebrations of birthdays or attending funerals.

Franta is ninety, and does not talk much about the past, but in the company of Mukls he often makes jokes. They had in common a profound sense of humor that was woven into every conversation. Franta is also the only Mukl with whom I maintain ongoing contact during the year. At least once a month we exchange e-mails; he often sends me news about the Mukl community or photos from their gatherings. Afraid that it may never be possible for him to read what I am writing, I decided to read him parts of this book. He listened to my struggle to translate the English text to Czech and then just nodded while I read. Many times he interrupted and began to talk about what happened. Usually it is hard to get him to talk about Muklhood or the past. When I met him for the first time, he made lunch for me at his place and talked about his wife, who had recently died. He was not very open to talk about his Mukl-hood before he met his wife.

Reading my text to him changed something. Perhaps he finally began to really trust me. Over the last years we have become close friends. Franta was not easy to interview. He was very uncomfortable talking about what happened and about himself. Compared to others, Franta's interviews were short, formal, and generally unsatisfying. But, ironically, we became, over time, close friends and keep in touch. Franta lives in his apartment alone and his computer and car keep him connected to others, mostly Mukls.

Individual forms of reconciliation are one's everyday efforts to bear the tensions. One's everyday condition combines recovery from facing death with the sense of tragedy embodied in future hope. Mukls' reconciliation is their daily coping with last night's dreams and tomorrow's possibilities. Whether it is through the weekly meetings in a restaurant like those at Café Ganys, annual returns to camps and prisons, birthday celebrations, or hospital visits, it is clear to me that reconnecting with family has become central to post-prison, post-1989 Muklhood.

When Mukls connect, they shake hands and hug, they greet one another, they talk, or they share all in silence. In their depth and in their affection, acts of mutual care transcend the boundaries of traditional Czech friendships. In a tragic way, their silent togetherness, their joking and talking are shared moments in their habitus, all they have left now at the twilight of Muklhood.

Conclusion

My intention was to carefully investigate the gap between what was experienced, remembered, and reconciled by people who had been a threat to the state's pursuit of a political fiction. The challenge was to represent social suffering without its being overshadowed by individual and communal experiences of violent events. Individual narratives of former political prisoners and my observations of Mukls' social life became the primary ethnographic data for this book. I have also included data based on Mukls' written narratives, documentary films and my archival studies. I have done so in order to show the ways in which Mukls relate to Czech society, and to emphasize both their past experiences and their present politics.

My early research questions evolved from my interest in the Mukls' past.

I pursued the reconstruction of the Mukls' past through the investigation of their voice. I applied a model of discourse analysis and treated the Mukls' narratives as a text. While comparing individual narratives, I began to see Mukls' shared patterns. Mukls' narratives show speech patterns signifying the transformation of kinship relatedness, citizenship and the formation of their community through the space of death; they refer to their community as a family. It became evident that individual struggles under the state's strategic violence led to the development of new forms of social structures. The process of state-organized, systematic liquidation of any political opposition led to the making of a new community, the Mukl family. Members of the Mukl family share the experience of having lived through the Communist, Stalinist, silencing rituals not only practiced after arrest in institutions such as prisons, courts, and labor camps, but also after the Mukls returned to their homes. My aim was to illustrate the formation of this family, and discuss bonding experiences such as joking relations, but also modes of fragmentation of this new family.

The state's strategic oppression of kinship and citizenship ties clashed with the prisoners' adaptation to a new relatedness. I found that, as they redefined their notion of kinship and citizenship, they opened a real possibility for future hope. Mukls testified that the state, under the Communist political system, tried to distort their ways of belonging to state and to family. I have discussed these relationships as relatedness. From the Mukls' narratives that I gathered, it is evident that they accomplished a transformation of their relatedness. While developing the argument about relatedness, I also learned that the Mukl family, bound by mutual solidarity, shared experiences of suffering and a language, is not a homogeneous family. Mukls' shared experience of violent rituals gives them a consciousness of togetherness, but, at the same time, I see fragmentations within the Mukl community.

Since 1995, when I met the Mukls, I recognized that it was necessary to address, in addition to Mukls' past, a representation of Muklhood as lived today. I have come to the conclusion that central to Muklhood today is the Mukls' everyday effort to come to terms with the past. This I have identified as reconciliation. Today they are striving to recover their voices as individuals and, at the same time, as a community. To come to terms with the past, they are defining a new language, the language of reconciliation. The stories as told by Mukls and Muklyněs is a composition of not only many clear and sharp images of struggle for survival, but also images with a sense of time and space distorted by violence. Their narratives express the paradoxical relationship between the ideas of prison and home, lost kinship and new family, solidarity and fragmentation, citizenship and betrayal, tragedy and humor, morality and fiction. This paradigm shaped Mukls' subjectivity.

I have discussed subjectivity in distinct ways. Mukls' faces, in my written and visual representation, emerged from analysis and became the thread running through my narratives. I have discussed face in the context of Mukls' lost and denied face when they were arrested, interrogated, put on trial and imprisoned in the camps and also in the context of their later recovery of face in reconciliation. When writing about face, I refer to the ability to speak, to communicate, as well as to visibility. When Mukls were arrested they felt they were made invisible, they were defaced from the public eye. Returning to Jáchymov means reclaiming face. My photographs are, in a way, reclaiming Mukls' face, but also giving face to those who have become the figures in the archives. Making portraits was a way for me to illuminate individual stories of desire for "political truth." I refer to the concept of political truth established by intellectual voices in Central and Eastern Europe, particularly Václav Havel, as a means of confronting the totalitarian political system of the Communist state.

One of the outcomes of this book is an understanding that the process of reconciliation is an act of recovering Mukls' face. Restoring Mukls' face is a counteraction to Mukls' defacement by the state. The process of defacement of the Mukls shaped the ways in which they see themselves. When Mukls retell their stories, images of specific situations emerge: Čeněk's last image of his mother during his arrest, the image of Mukls marching in the bus and looking through the glass at the eclipse, or a Mukl father spending forbidden time with his children by looking through the window of their bedroom. In their narratives Mukls revealed the visual patterns embodied in the very condition of Muklhood. The sense of vision is built into the structure of their passage. The power exercised by the StB over the political other included manipulating the visual sense as a means of controlling the Mukls' pain and depersonalization by acts of torture.

I proposed the concept of violent ritual, the space of death, as a conceptual framework for the examination of historical events, which gave rise to the formation of a significant relationship between the state and the politically oppressed. Three specific events: arrest, interrogation, and trial show in detail that these events, while they have their locus in historical time and place, also have a fluid character. The Mukls' arrests, interrogations and later their trials were events inseparable from the larger context, a totalitarian form of political power. I showed how, in very concrete ways, while political power such as that utilized by totalitarianism intensely reinforced and transformed its ideological fiction into everydayness, it was countered by the power of Mukls' relatedness. Ultimately totalitarian political practices impacted relatedness within Czechoslovak society as a whole.

I have discussed how institutionalized violent rituals impacted on the early formations of Mukls' subjectivities. I have tried to understand what it means to be a Mukl, how Mukls' subjectivity is redefined over time and space. I showed the power of relatedness while exposing a type of political, strategic isolation experienced by the prisoners as social exclusion from society, a condition strategically enforced by the state, and the prisoners' ability to form new types of relationships within that strategic isolation.

Today Mukls are returning to the very same "hells" they once endured, the prisons, courtrooms, factories, mines and work camps to remember, to be together, to call for justice for one regime's crimes which are rooted in the forced living of a fiction. The desire for justice is central to the Mukls' language of reconciliation. During their conversations they return to the subject of justice. They are turning to the institution of the state and asking for the judicial system to create space for the acknowledgment of the terrible mistake through which they were forced to live. Mukls' language of reconciliation is not just the return to the old and familiar. It is walking together again in the space of suffering, creating narratives about the past, celebrating survival, silent remembering of victims, shaking hands, embracing shoulders, sharing meals, exchanging jokes, and resisting denial of the darkness of the Communist concentration camps. It is also the mirror of an everyday effort to overcome the trauma and pain of intended liquidation, rejection, and alienation. Finally, I have also argued that while the tragic and unfortunate past continues to haunt the Mukls', they maintain hope for the future through their invention of a new language of reconciliation.

I conclude that a Mukl or Muklyně, the subject of liquidation, is a man or woman who speaks of reconciliation. In their language of reconciliation, memory, time and place intersect. In their narratives they talk about different ways they had to negotiate the social web of imprisonment, not only in a Communist concentration camp, but also after release. The political other became a Mukl or Muklyně, a member of a new family, a community whose language was shaped by the individual and collective experience of culturally specific violence.

In the post-totalitarian state the Mukl, the political other from the previous political regime, remains an other through distinct desires and acts of coming to terms with the experience of organized violence. Like most members of the Czech and Slovak states, former prisoners are now facing the post-totalitarian remaking of life. In contrast to society at large, the political prisoners' recovery from the totalitarian past has proved that the ethics of political life and individual coming to terms with the past are closely related and crucial to their efforts towards reconciliation. For Mukls, and others who suffered under the Communist regime, the struggle for truth is the struggle for justice protected by law. Mukls' language of reconciliation is a condition of remaking life after trauma, a process of communication which has many verbal as well as nonverbal components. The Mukls' dilemmas are rooted in their desire for rehabilitation and their hope to be understood. Their struggle to find a way to tell their story is complicated and central to the Mukls' condition today. Mukls' communication about their condition is marked by the injustice that is embodied in being forced to live a fiction produced by ideology. Their language of reconciliation is the property of individuals as well as the shared property of the Mukls' community. Mukls' reconciliation is their daily coping with last night's dreams. As they continue to struggle to recover their truth about violence in their pasts, everyday is marked by their having faced death and by their need to maintain hope for recovery of their lost voice.

The annual public meetings and ordinary small visits are Mukl occasions during which they express the strength of their family ties and call for the acknowledgment of deeply felt injustice. Mukls' forms of reconciling: returning, celebrating, remembering, and relating are reinforced through social gatherings, and their solidarity is more effective than their search for justice in courtrooms because they allow for communal reconstruction of experiences of violence. I read these ordinary visits and extraordinary annual celebrations as both small and large, rich, multilayered texts containing a register of Mukls' relatedness and their claim of self. In this historical context, one long-term consequence of those processes was the creation of a distinct new community, the community of the state's political others. In Czechoslovakia the Mukls (that is the title they bear in common, political other) became just such a new community. Muklhood, the tragic condition of lived political fiction, has now, at the end of Mukls' lives, turned for some Mukls into life with a deep sense of connectedness to others, to fellow Mukls.

References

Agamben, Giorgio
   1995   *Homo Sacer*. San Francisco: Stanford University Press.
   2000   Means without End: Notes on Politics. Minneapolis: University of Minnesota Press.

Agar, Michael
   1994   Language Shock. New York: Quill.
   1996   The Professional Stranger. San Diego: Academic Press.

Amin, Shahid
   1995   Event, Metaphor, Memory. Berkeley: University of California Press.

Anderson, Benedict
   1991   Imagined Communities. London: Verso.

Applebaum, Anne
   2003   Gulag: A History. New York: Doubleday.

Arendt, Hannah
   1966   The Origins of Totalitarianism. New York: Harcourt, Brace and World, Inc.

Aretxaga, Begona
   1997   Shattering Silence. Princeton, New Jersey: Princeton University Press.

Asad, Talal
   1997   On Torture, or Cruel, Inhumane, and Degrading Treatment. In Social Suffering. Veena Das, Arthur Kleinman, and Margaret Lock Eds. Pp. 285–308. Berkeley: University of California Press.

Babka, Lukaš, and Václav Veber, Eds.
   2002   *Za svobodu a demokracii*. (For Freedom and Democracy). Hradec Králové, Hradec Králové University.

Bakhtin, Mikhail
1996   Discourse in the Novel: The Dialogic Imagination. Austin: University of
        Texas Press.

Banks, Marcus, and Howard Morphy, Eds.
1999   Rethinking Visual Anthropology. New Haven: Yale University Press.

Bareilly, John
1993   Nationalism and the State. Manchester: Manchester University Press.

Bartošek, Karel
2001   *Český Vězeň.* (Czech Prisoners). Prague: Paseka.

Bednářová, Marta
2000   *K Mrtvým se Na Čaj nechodí.* (Dead People Are Not Hosting You for a
        Cup of Tea). Prague: KOKOS.

Bell, Catherine
1997   Ritual: Perspectives and Dimensions. New York: Oxford University
        Press.

Boas, Franz
1925   Social Organization and the Secret Societies of Kwakiutl Indians. Wash-
        ington, DC: American National Museum.

Bouška, Tomaš and Klára Pinerová
2009   Czechoslovak Political Prisoners. European Union.

Brinton, William M., and Alan Rinzler, Eds.
1990   Without Force or Lies. San Francisco: Mercury House.

Brodský, Jaroslav
1971   Solution Gamma. Toronto: Gamma Print.

Bubeníčková-Kuthanová, Milena
1991   *Vybledlá Fotografie.* (Faded Photograph). Prague: Vyšehrad.

Cavel, Stanley
1997   Comments on Veena Das's essay Language and Body: Transactions in
        the Construction of Pain. In Social Suffering. Veena Das, Arthur Klein-
        man, and Margaret Locke, Eds. Pp. 93–98. Berkeley: University of
        California Press.

Černý, Václav
1994   *V Zúženém Prostoru.* (In a Narrow Space). Prague: Souvislosti.

Chatterjee, Parthia
1993   The Nation and Its Fragments: Colonial and Post-Colonial Histories.
        Princeton: Princeton University Press.

Chytil, Václav
2003   *Uranové Doly.* (Uranium Mines). Praha: Universita Karlova.

References   147

Comaroff, John L.
1995   Perspectives on Nationalism and War. Luxembourg: Gordon and Breach
       Publishers.

Courtois, Stephane, Nicolas Werth, Jean-Louis Panne, Andrzej Paczkowski, Karel
Bartosek, and Jean-Louis Margolin, Eds.
1999   Černá Kniha Komunismu. (The Black Book of Communism).
       Prague: Paseka.

Daniel, E. Valentine
1996   Charred Lullabies: Chapters in an Anthropology of Violence. Princeton,
       NJ: Princeton University Press.
1997   Mood, Moment, and Mind. In Violence and Subjectivity. Veena Das,
       Arthur Kleinman, Mamphela Ramphele, and Pamela Reynolds, Eds. Pp.
       333–366. Berkeley: University of California Press.
1997   Suffering Nation and Alienation. In Social Suffering. Veena Das, Arthur
       Kleinman, and Margaret Lock, Eds. Pp. 309–358. Berkeley: University
       of California Press.

Das, Veena
1995   Critical Events: An Anthropological Perspective on Contemporary
       India. New York: Oxford University Press.
1997   Language and Body: Transactions in the Constructions of Pain. In Social
       Suffering. Veena Das, Arthur Kleinman, and Margaret Lock, Eds. Pp. ix–
       xxvii. Berkeley: University of California Press.
2000   The Act of Witnessing: Violence, Poisonous Knowledge, and Subjectivity.
       In Violence and Subjectivity. Veena Das, Arthur Kleinman, Mamphela
       Ramphele, and Pamela Reynolds, Eds. Pp. 205–225. Berkeley: University
       of California Press.
2007   Life and Words: Violence and the Descent into the Ordinary. Berkeley:
       University of California Press.

Das, Veena, and Arthur Kleinman
2000   Introduction. In Violence and Subjectivity. Veena Das, Arthur Kleinman,
       Mamphela Ramphele, and Pamela Reynolds, Eds. Pp. 1–18. Berkeley:
       University of California Press.
2001   Introduction. In Remaking a World. Veena Das, Arthur Kleinman, Mar-
       garet Lock, Mamphela Ramphele, and Pamela Reynolds, Eds. Pp. 1–30.
       Berkeley: University of California Press.

Das, Veena, and Deborah Poole, Eds.
2004   Anthropology in the Margins of the State. Santa Fe: School of American
       Research Press.

Desjarlais, Robert
1992   Body and Emotion: The Aesthetics of Illness and Healing in the Nepal
       Himalayas. Philadelphia: University of Pennsylvania Press.

Donnelly, Jack
    2003   Universal Human Rights in Theory and Practice. Ithaca: Cornell University Press.

Dušek, Radim, and Marie Macková
    1996   *Osudy Politických Vežnů* 1948–1989. (Fate of the Political Prisoners 1948–1989). Usti nad Orlici: State Regional Archive.

Dvořák, Bohdan, Ed.
    1991   International Conference about the Crimes of Communism. Pardubice: *Ústav Veterinarni Osvety.*

Dvořáková, Zora
    2001   *O Miladě Horákové.* (About Milada Horak). Prague: Nakladatelstvi Eva.

Emerson, Robert M., Rachel I. Fretz, and Linda L. Shaw
    1995   Writing Ethnographic Fieldnotes. London: The University of Chicago Press.

Epstein, Helen
    1988   Children of the Holocaust: Conversations with Sons and Daughters of Survivors. New York: Penguin Books.

Evans-Pritchard, E. E.
    1940   The Nuer. New York: Oxford Clarendon Press.

Fawn, Rick
    2000   The Czech Republic: A Nation of Velvet. Harwood Academic Publishers.

Feierabend, Ladislav
    1988   *Soumrak Československé Demokracie.* (Czech Democracy at Dusk). London: Rozmluvy.

Feitlowitz, Marguerite
    1998   A Lexicon of Terror: Argentina and the Legacies of Torture. Oxford: Oxford University Press.

Feldman, Allen
    1991   Formations of Violence. Chicago: The University of Chicago Press.

Fortes, Meyer, and E. E. Evans-Pritchard, Eds.
    1940   African Political Systems. London: Oxford University Press.

Foucault, Michel
    1972   The Archaeology of Knowledge. New York: Pantheon.
    1977   Discipline and Punish. New York: Vintage.

Gal, Susan
    1987   Code-switching and Consciousness on the European Periphery. American Ethnologist 14 (4):637–653.

Gal, Susan, and Gail Kligman
    2000   The Politics of Gender after Socialism. Princeton: Princeton University Press.

Gal, Susan, and Gail Kligman, Eds.
2000   Reproducing Gender: Politics, Publics, and Everyday Life after Socialism. Princeton: Princeton University Press.

Gavras, Costa
1970   The Confession. French-Italian dramatic film, 135 min. Paramount Pictures.

Geertz, Clifford
1973   The Interpretation of Cultures. New York: Basic Books.
1995   After the Fact. Cambridge: Harvard University Press

Gellner, Ernest
1983   Nations and Nationalisms. Ithaca, New York: Cornell University Press.
1994   Encounters with Nationalism. Oxford: Blackwell.

Gluckman, Max
1965   Politics, Law and Ritual in Tribal Society. Oxford: Basil Blackwell.

Goffman, Erving
1961   Asylums. New York: Anchor Books.
1974   Frame Analysis. Boston: Northeastern University Press.

Gramsci, Antonio
1971   Selections from the Prison Notebooks. New York: International Publishers.

Greenhouse, Carol J.
1996   A Moment's Notice: Time Politics across Cultures. Ithaca: Cornell University Press.

Grimshaw, Anna
2001   The Ethnographer's Eye. Cambridge: Cambridge University Press.

Gruntorad, Jiří, and Petr Uhl
1990   O *Československém Vězeňství/Sbornik Charty 77.* (About Czechoslovakian Prisoners/A Memorial Volume, Charter 77). Prague: Orbis.

Guha, Ranajit
1999   Elementary Aspects of Peasant Insurgency in Colonial India. Durham: Duke University Press.
2000   On Some Aspects of the Historiography of Colonial India. In Mapping Subaltern Studies and the Postcolonial. Vinayak Chaturvedi, Ed. Pp. 1–7. London: Verso.

Guha, Ranajit, Ed.
1997   Chandra's Death. In A Subaltern Studies Reader 1986–1995. Ranajit Guha, Ed. Pp. 34–62. Minneapolis: University of Minnesota Press.

Guha, Ranajit, and Gayatri Chakrovorty Spivak
1988   Preface. In Selected Subaltern Studies. Guha Ranajit and Gayatri Chakrovorty Spivak, Eds. Pp. 35–36. New York: Oxford University Press.

Gumperz, John J.
1971   Language in Social Groups; Essays by John J. Gumperz Selected and
        Introduced by Anwar S. Dil. Stanford: Stanford University Press.

Halliday, M. A. K.
1978   Language as Social Semiotic. London: Edward Arnold.

Havel, Václav
1989   *Do Ruzných Stran.* (Toward Different Directions). Prague: KLN.
1990   The Power of the Powerless. In Without Force or Lies. William M. Briton
        and Alan Rinzler, Eds. Pp. 43–127. San Francisco: Mercury House, In-
        corporated.
1995   *O Lidskou Identitu.* (About Human Identity). London: Rozmluvy.
1997   The Art of the Impossible. Paul Wilson et al., trans. New York: Knopf.

Hegel, G .W. F.
1977   Phenomenology of Spirit, translated by A.V. Miller. London: Oxford
        University Press.

Hejl, Vilém and Karel Kaplan
1986   *Pravda o Organizovaném Násilí.* (Report on Organized Oppression).
        Toronto: Sixty-Eight Publishers Corporation.

Holubová, Miloslava
1998   *Cestou Necestou.* (Off the Path, The Path). Prague: Torst.

Holy, Ladislav
1996   The Little Czech and the Great Czech Nation: National Identity and the
        Post-Communist Social Transformation. Cambridge: Cambridge Univer-
        sity Press.

Hymes, Dell
1974   Foundations in Sociolinguistics. Philadelphia: University Press.

Ješ, Jiří
1997   *Co Přines Čas.* (What Time Gives). Prague: Academia.

Justman, Zuzana
2000   A Trial in Prague (documentary film 58 min.). New York: The Cinema
        Guild, Inc.

Kafka, Franz
1937   The Trial. New York: Schocken Books.

Kantůrková, Eva
1987   *Přitelkyne z Domu Smutku.* (Friend from the House of Sadness).
        Prague: Československý Spisovatel.

Kaplan, Karel
1989   *Mocní a Bezmocní.* (The Powerful and the Powerless). Toronto: Sixty-
        Eight Publishers.
1990   *Pravda O Československsku 1945–1948.* (The Truth about Czechoslovakia
        1945–1948). Prague: Panorama.

2002   *StB o Sobě*. (The StB about Itself). Prague: Department of Documentation of the Crimes of Communism.

Kaplan, Karel, and Vladimir Pacl
1993   *Tajný Prostor Jáchymov*. (Secret Space Jáchymov). České Budějovice: ACTYS.

Kennan, George
1958   Siberia and the Exile System. The University of Chicago Press.

Kleinman, Arthur and Veena Das, Eds.
2001   Introduction. In Remaking a World. Veena Das, Arthur Kleinman, Margaret Lock, Mamphela Ramphele, and Pamela Reynolds, Eds. Pp. 1–30. Berkeley: University of California Press.

Kleinman, Arthur, Veena Das, and Margaret Lock, Eds.
1997   Introduction. In Social Suffering. Veena Das, Arthur Kleinman, and Margaret Lock, Eds. Pp. ix–xxvii. Berkeley: University of California Press.

Kmet, J. J.
1972   Maturita Zivota. Czechoslovakia: Susice, unpublished.

Krajina, Vladimír
1991   *Vysoká Hra*. (A High Game). Prague: Nakladatelstvi Eva.

Kroča, Květoslav
2003   *Jáchymovské Peklo*. (Jáchymov Hell). Prague: Mirror Promotion s.r.o.

Kuklová-Jisová, Božena
2002   *Krasná něma paní*. (Our Beautiful Lady). Prague: Nakladateltsvi(c) ARSCI.

Kundera, Milan
1967   *Žert*. (The Joke). Prague: Československý Spisovatel.

Langer, Lawrence L.
1991   The Ruins of Memory. New Haven: Yale University Press.

Leach, E. R.
1964   Political Systems of Highland Burma. The Athlone Press.
1976   Culture and Communication. Cambridge: Cambridge University Press.

Leff, Carol Skalnik
1996   The Czech and Slovak Republics: Nation versus State. Boulder: Westview Press.

Lesák, Josef
2000   *Čas Oponou Trhnul*. (Time Pulled Away the Stage Curtain). Prague: Fortuna.

Limon, Jose E.
1994   Dancing with the Devil. Madison: The University of Wisconsin Press.

Loebl, Eugen
1976   My Mind on Trial. New York: A Helen and Kurt Wolff Book.

London, Arthur
1968   *Doznaní.* (The Confession). (L' aveu). Prague: Ceskoslovensky Spisovatel.

Lukeš, Jan
1998   Testimony in the Tower of Death. Kristina Vlachova. CZ TV 58 Betach, Praha.

Majer, Jiří
1995   *Cestou k Demokracii.* (The Path to Democracy). Příbram: Museum Třetího Odboje and KPV.

Malinowski, Bronislaw
1954   Magic, Science, and Religion and Other Essays. New York: A Doubleday Anchor Book.

Maloumian, Armand
1991   *Synove Gulagu.* (Sons of the Gulag). Prague: Konsultace.

Marcus, George E., and Michael M. J. Fischer
1999   Anthropology as Cultural Critique. Chicago: The University of Chicago Press.

Mead, Margaret, and Gregory Bateson
1942   Balinese Character: A Photographic Analysis. New York Academy of Sciences, Special Publications 2. New York: New York Academy of Sciences.

Mňačko, Ladislav
1963   *Opozděné Reportáže.* (Late Reportage). Prague: NPL.

Morris, David.
1997   About Suffering: Voice, Genre, and Moral Community. In Social Suffering. Veena Das, Arthur Kleinman, and Margaret Locke, Eds. Pp. 25–46. Berkeley: University of California Press.

Mucha, Jiří
1967   Living and Partly Living. New York: McGraw-Hill Book Company.
1970   *Studené Slunce.* (Cold Sun). Prague: Československý spisovatel.

Nader, Laura
2002   The Life of the Law. Berkeley: University of California Press.

National Film Archive
2005   Czech Television (CT24) film clip from Narodni Film Archiv 2005.

Němeček, Milan
1998   *Mašinove.* (The Mašin Family). Prague: Torst.

Novák, Rudolf
1991   *Svatá spověd Esténbáka.* (The Holy Confession of an StB Guy). Prague: Lirekan.

Oliva, Otmar
2002   *Bytem v hrůze.* (To Live in Horror). Velehrad: Ottobre 12.

Orlove, Benjamin
1994   The Dead Policemen Speak: Power, Fear, and Narrative in the 1931 Molloccahua Killing (Cusco). In Unruly Order, Violence, Power, and Cultural Identity in the High Provinces of Southern Peru. Deborah Poole, Ed. Pp. 32–62. Denver: Westview Press.

Palivec, Josef
1996   *Prózy/Listy z vězení/Pozdravy přátel.* (Poems/Letters from Prisoners/ Greetings from Friends). Prague: Torst.

Pálkosková-Weisenbergerová, Albína
1991   *Nebyl to Jen Sen.* (It Wasn't Just a Dream). Prague: Luxpress.

Pandey, Gyanendra
1988   Peasant Revolt and Indian Nationalism. In Selected Subaltern Studies. Ranajit Guha and Gayatri Chakravorty Spivak, Eds. Pp. 233–287. Oxford: Oxford University Press.
1997   In Defense of the Fragment; Writing about Hindu-Muslim Riots in India Today. In A Subaltern Studies Reader 1986–1995. Ranajit Guha, Ed. Pp. 34–62. Minneapolis: University of Minnesota Press.
2000   Voices from the Edge; the Struggle to Write Subaltern Histories. In Mapping Subaltern Studies in the Post-Colonial. Vinayak Chaturvedi, Ed. Pp. 281–299. New York: Verso.
2001   Remembering Partition. Cambridge: Cambridge University Press.

Palouš, Radim
1999   *Hovory's Havly.* (Conversations with the Havels). Středoluky: Zdeněk Susa.

Pecka, Karel
1968   *Na co Umírají Muži.* (What Men are Dying From). Prague: Mlada Fronta.
1980   *Motáky Nezvěstné mu.* (Smuggled Letters to the Disappeared). Toronto: Sixty-Eight Publishers.
1991   *Veliký Slunovrat.* (Big Eclipse). Prague: Pra(c)ced.

Pehe, Jiří
2002   *Vytunelovaná Demokracie.* ("Tunneled" Democracy). Prague: Academia.

Pejskar, Jožka
1987   *Pronásledovaní vlastenci.* (Persecuted Patriots). Samizdat, USA.

Petrašová, Ludmila
2002   *Vězeňské Tábory v Jáchymovských Uranových Dolech.* In Za svobodu a Democracii (For the Freedom and Democracy). Lukaš Babka and Václav Weber, Eds. Pp. 54–75. Hradec Kralove: Europské Hnutí v České Republice.

Pithart, Petr
1990   *Osmašedesátý.* (Sixty eight). Prague: Rozmluvy.

Poole, Deborah
1997   Vision Race, and Modernity. Princeton: Princeton University Press.

Poole, Deborah, Ed.
1994   Peasant Culture and Political Violence in the Peruvian Andes: Sendero Luminoso and the State. In Unruly Order: Violence, Power, and Cultural Identity in the High Provinces of Southern Peru. Deborah Poole, Ed. Pp. 224–247. Denver: Westview Press.

Pospisil, Leopold
1971   Anthropology of Law and Comparative Theory. New York: Harper and Row Publishers.

Rambousek, Ota
1991   *Jenom Ne Strach.* (Not Only Fear). Vimberk: Nezavislé Tiskové Středisko.

Rejali, Darius M.
1994   Torture and Modernity. Denver: Westview Press, Inc.

Reynolds, Pamela
2000   The Ground of All Making: State Violence, the Family, and Political Activists. In Violence and Subjectivity. Veena Das, Arthur Kleinman, Mamphela Ramphele, and Pamela Reynolds, Eds. Pp. 141–170. Berkeley: University of California Press.

Roseberry, William.
1989   Anthropologies and Histories. New Brunswick: Rutgers University Press.

Rosenberg, Tina
1992   Children of Cain. New York: Penguin Books.

Ross, Fiona C.
2001   Speech and Silence: Women's Testimony in the First Five Weeks of Public Hearings of the South African Truth and Reconciliation Commission. In Remaking the World. Veena Das, Arthur Kleinman, Margaret Lock, Mampela Ramphele, and Pamela Reynolds, Eds. Pp. 250–280. Berkeley: University of California Press.
2003   Bearing Witness: Women and the Truth and Reconciliation Commission in South Africa. London: Pluto Press.

Rotrekl, Zdeněk
1991   *Sněhem zaváte vinobraní.* (Snowfall Covers the Wine Harvest). Brno: Atlantis.
2001   *Světlo přichazí potmě.* (Light Is Coming from the Dark). Brno: Atlantis.

Ruby, Jay, Ed.
1982   A Crack in the Mirror. Philadelphia: University of Pennsylvania Press.

Ruby, Jay
2000   Picturing Culture: Explorations of Film and Anthropology. Chicago: University of Chicago Press.

Rupnik, Jacques
2002   *Dějiny Komunistické Strany Československske.* (History of the Communist Party of Czechoslovakia). Prague: Academia.
1995   The Post-Totalitarian Blues. Journal of Democracy 6(2): 61–73.

Salgado, Sebastio
2000   The Children. New York: Aperture.

Scarry, Elaine
1985   The Body in Pain. New York: Oxford University Press.

Šedivý, František
2002   *Pod věži smrti*. (Under the Tower of Death). Prague: Nakladatelstvi Eva.

Šedivý, Zdeněk
2003   *Uranový Gulag*. (Uranium Gulag). Brno: Moba.

Schulz, William F., Ed.
2007   The Phenomenon of Torture. Philadephia: University of Pennsylvania Press.

Šimková, Dagmar
1994   *Byly jsme tam taky*. (We Were There, Too). Prague: Orbis.

Školoud, Lubomír, and Petr Štěpánek
1992   *Na všechno bud připraven*. (Be Ready for Anything). Hradec Králove: Kruh.

Škvorecký, Josef
1990   *Mirakl*. (The Miracle). Brno: Atlantis.

Slyomovics, Susan
1998   The Object of Memory. Philadelphia: University of Pennsylvania Press.

Solzhenitsyn, Aleksandr
1971   For the Good of the Cause. New York: Praeger.
1974   Gulag Archipelago. New York: Harper and Row.
1991   One Day in the Life of Ivan Denisovich. New York: Noonday Press.

Sontag, Susan
2004   Regarding the Torture of Others. New York Times Magazine, May 23.

Spivak, Gayatri Chakravorty
1988   Can the Subaltern Speak? In Marxism and the Interpretation of Culture. Gary Nelson and Lawrence Grosseberg, Eds. Pp. 271–313. Urbana: University of Illinois Press.

Steward, Julian
1955   Theory of Cultural Change. Urbana: University of Illinois Press.

Stone, Linda
2001   New Directions in Anthropological Kinship. Lanham, MD: Rowman & Littlefield Publisher, INC.

Swartz, Marc, Victor Turner, and Arthur Tuden, Eds.
1966   Political Anthropology. New York: Aldine Publishing Company.

Táborský, Edward
1970   Communism in Czechoslovakia 1948–1960. Princeton: Princeton U. Press.

Taussig, Michael T.
   1987   Shamanism, Colonialism, and the Wild Man. Chicago: The University of Chicago Press.
   1999   Defacement. San Francisco: Stanford University Press.

Tigrid, Pavel
   1982   *Dnešek je Váš zítřek je náš*. (Today Is Yours, Tomorow Is Ours). Prague: Vokno.

Timmerman, Jacobo
   2002   Prisoner without a Name, Cell without a Number. Madison: University of Wisconsin Press.

Todeschini, Maya
   2001   The Bomb's Womb? Women and the Atom Bomb. In Remaking a World. Veena Das, Arthur Kleinman, Margaret Lock, Mamphela Ramphele, and Pamela Reynolds, Eds. Pp. 102–156. Berkeley: University of California Press.

Trnka, Susanna
   2008   State of Suffering: Political Violence and Community Survival in Fiji. Ithaca, NY: Cornell University Press.

Turner, Victor
   1969   The Ritual Process. Ithaca: Cornell University Press.

Vaško, Václav
   1990   Kronika Katholické Církve v Ceskoslovenku po Druhé Světové Válce I.&II. Chronicle of Catholic Church in Czechoslovakia after WW II. I.& II.
   1999   *Ne všim jsem byl rad*. (Not All I Did Was Fun). Prague: Karmelitanske(c) Nakladatelstvi.

Verdery, Katherine
   1989   Transnationalism, Nationalism, Citizenship, and Property: Eastern Europe since 1989. American Ethnologist 25(2):291–306.
   1996   What Was Socialism and What Comes Next? Princeton: Princeton University Press.

Vincent, Joan
   1990   Anthropology and Politics. Tuscon: The University of Arizona Press.

Visweswaran, Kamala
   1996   Small Speeches, Subaltern Gender: Nationalist Ideology and Its Historiography. In Selected Subaltern Studies IX. Pp. 83–125. New York: Oxford University Press.

Vlachová, Kristina
   2002   The Tower of Death: A Chapter from the Current Justice. CZ TV-58-Betakam, Prague.

Warren, Kay B.
  2000   Mayan Multiculturalism and the Violence of Memories. In Violence and Subjectivity. Veena Das, Arthur Kleinman, Mamphela Raphael, and Pamela Reynolds, Eds. Pp. 296–314. Berkeley: University of California Press.

Wheaton, Bernard and Zdeněk Kavan
  1992   The Velvet Revolution. Denver: Westview Press.

Woodward, Susan L.
  2000   Violence-Prone Area or International Transition? Adding the Role of Outsiders in Balkan Violence. In Violence and Subjectivity. Veena Das, Arthur Kleinman, Mamhela Ramphele, and Pamela Reynolds, Eds. Pp. 19–45. Berkeley: University of California Press.

Index

About the Author

Jana Kopelentova Rehak is an assistant professor of anthropology at Loyola University, Maryland, in Baltimore and an affiliate at Towson University in Towson, Maryland. She received her doctoral degree from the anthropology department at American University in Washington, D.C., her MFA from the University of Delaware in Newark, and a BA from the Academy of Performing Arts in Prague, the Czech Republic.

Her research specializations include Central Eastern Europe as well as urban North America. In Central Eastern Europe her research is focused on political life, aging, migration, minorities, language, visual culture, and ecology. In the United States she practices applied anthropology of urban life focused on housing, education, health, migration, environment, and public art in Baltimore.

Her background in cultural anthropology and the visual arts has shaped her multidisciplinary perspective on the social sciences and humanities.